BIBBY'S

MORE GOOD FOOD

DIANNE BIBBY

CONTENTS

FOREWORD

In the world of culinary artistry, there exists a realm where every detail is a brushstroke on the canvas of flavour, where moments are captured not only with taste but through the enchantment of colour and light. In this extraordinary cookbook, *Bibby's – More Good Food*, Dianne takes us on a journey where her mastery of both the kitchen and the art of storytelling and photography will leave you feeling not just inspired, but deeply connected.

I've had the privilege of sitting at many tables with Dianne, and I can attest that she embodies the essence of simplicity in the basics, while never shying away from appreciating the slightly more and lush. Her love for bringing people together around a table is evident on every page, where her ability to make you feel cared for and safe is nothing short of magical.

This cookbook is a symphony of flavours, thoughtfully organized into chapters that include the essentials of the pantry, the warm embrace of breads, the delight of morning treats, vibrant and plant-rich salads and sides, the artistry of both quick and slow plates, her enchanting world of baking, and cocktails that are simply to die for. Evidently, the meticulous writing of each recipe shows the time that went into creating, testing and capturing each dish.

We embark on culinary journeys and create cookbooks for various reasons, but Dianne reminds us that it's not about seeing our name on a shelf or selling thousands of copies. It's about sharing the joy of creating and caring. In *Bibby's – More Good Food*, we not only share her recipes but also accept the beauty found on every page. It's a gift to be able to do this, and an even greater gift to appreciate the beauty in every bite, in every colour, and in every shared moment. Welcome to a world where food becomes art, and art becomes a feast for the soul. Enjoy your journey through these beautiful pages because I just cannot get out of them!

– Jan Hendrik van der Westhuizen
MICHELIN-STAR CHEF

VISCERAL FOOD

There's nothing to writing. All you do is sit down at your typewriter and bleed.

– ERNEST HEMINGWAY

Our response to food is almost always visceral, an involuntary reaction borne from a gut feeling rather than a calculated or considered response. Guided by personal preference, we move towards that which pleasures the palate and enchants the senses. Sight, smell, taste and, funnily enough, sound, play an integral part in shaping our responses. Within the pentagon of taste – salt, sour, bitter, sweet and the current culinary obsession, umami, the savoury receptor – lies infinite permutations waiting to be discovered. And so our insatiable appetite for innovative food is fuelled and appeased. If you're after food less ordinary, come with me ...

After my first book, I thought I'd hang up the apron and yet, I'm here again, entangled in a web of words, trying to articulate the ever-changing voice of food in a way that is original, relevant and, above all else, deliciously memorable. When thinking about the storyline for my second book, I naturally referred to the first, re-reading it for the hundredth time. I realized my narrative hasn't changed at all. There's simply no substitute for the beautiful coming together over food. I believed it then, as I do now. Food is the least pretentious vehicle to connecting people. It shows up faithfully for all our miracle moments, triumphs and defeats, the heart-warming welcomes and sorrowful farewells. It's a nourisher and natural healer. It charms, captivates and delights. It is theatre. It is art. We never tire of it, do we? Fuelled by a fiery enthusiasm for inventiveness or, at best, a fresh take on the familiar, manipulated or spun in such a way as to disrupt the ordinary, cooking is a constant journey of discovery. Ruffling feathers and rousing an appetite for the unfamiliar can take us someplace wonderful. If you're stuck in the rut of repetitiveness, I hope this book will lure you into unexplored territories.

Cookbooks are so much more than just a compilation of recipes, measurements and methods. They are intimate stories and anecdotes of food as we experience it. If you read between the lines, you'll catch a glimpse of the cook and the finer nuances that depict culture, place and context. These are the stories I'm constantly inspired to tell. Escapism through food, whether literal or imagined, savoured for just the briefest moment in the company of one or many, is upliftment for the soul. To be a really good cook you need to be interested not only in food, but in people and life. It is this that keeps me coming back for more. These are the moments that feed the chase, the reason I continue to cook and write about food.

WHAT TO EXPECT

Devoid of intimidating complexities, the recipes are for the most part appealingly simple, versatile and straightforward. With the exception of perhaps several quirky characters, most ingredients are readily available, failing which, suitable stand-ins with similar traits are suggested. Far from being a temple of fine dining, this book embraces approachable food made with thoughtful consideration. Expect an abundance of textural contrast and funky flavour enhancers. Although small in stature, these big hitters can transform the mundane into the extraordinary. Hidden within the darkened corners of the pantry cupboard lies a treasure trove of possibilities. We delve into what constitutes a well-stocked pantry and how to maximize its potential to the fullest.

Many of the recipes are plant-centric without being exclusively vegetarian. There's a weighted leaning towards fresh, locally sourced produce, a movement I'm more than happy to get behind. Faddish trends are out. Resourcefulness, intuitive cooking and feel-good food are in.

The book is divided into nine vibrantly fresh and practical chapters that traverse borders and traditions, influenced largely by Middle Eastern and Mediterranean flavours. By no means do I claim authenticity to the recipes. They exist as loosely composed adaptations, diverging into modernistic terrains.

New to the book are The Golden Hour and Gathered Feasts, chapters I'm wildly excited about. We jump on the cocktail trend with herb-laced concoctions, fruit shrubs and a corruptive caramel liqueur. Salt rim the glasses and snag a seat at the bar.

In Gathered Feasts we throw open the doors to hospitality, marrying food and creative table-scaping in favour of intimate, at-home feasts. Our Moroccan table goes full tilt, while the others are slightly more casual, but equally special. The menus include a cohesive progression of flavours that work agreeably together. By no means are there hard and fast rules. Browse the chapters and compile a personalized menu, one that suits your mood, dietary preference or time constraints. You may want to trim it down from a full-scale dinner party to a simpler, kitchen-table supper. It can do that, too.

As is customary, we open with traditional breads and tasty nibbles or dips to pique the appetite and heighten expectations. If you're after a vegetarian menu, forgo the meat and swap for any one of the abundant salad options in the Well-Rooted chapter, or slot in an appetizer or two from the Mezze section. Dessert needn't be much nor perfect for that matter, although I afford this course the same affection and consideration as the preceding courses.

The recipes that follow have been hand-picked for their ability to challenge the comfortability of those culinary ruts we so often find ourselves in, visceral food that engages all the senses and stimulates an appetite for more good food.

When composing your guest list, invite some odd characters. Mix it up. Make new friends and stir up a flurry of excitement at your next dinner party.

HOW TO USE THIS BOOK

I've been known to speed read. Not so much novels, mostly non-fiction, cookbooks in particular. Casting one eye over the introductions, I flick through the pages until something grabs my attention. Using the image as a guideline, I head off in the general direction. Only when things go pear-shaped do I refer to the recipe to establish where the derailment occurred. Big mistake. Nowadays, I read the book, cover to cover, side-bar threads and cook's notes, the whole shebang. It is, after all, a condensed master class by the author, intended to help deliver the best possible version of itself. I suggest you do the same, unless of course, you like flying by the seat of your pants, like someone else I know.

Chapter grabbing is not only advised but strongly suggested. Flip from one to another, making full use of recipes that offer a willingness to be manipulated into more than one thing.

Make sure they put in a full shift to earn their keep. Drizzle a briny dressing (page 28) over steamed green beans or charred broccoli, then top with a handful of Toasty Seed Sprinkles (page 25). The Aubergine Caponata (page 16) lends instant personality to an impromptu cheese board or a casual thrown-together pasta salad. Savoury brunch recipes like the Za'atar Spanakopita (page 101) or Butternut & Swiss Chard Frittata (page 98) do a fine job filling in as lunch or light supper, with maybe a side salad or freshly baked bread. Flex your food muscles, adapt, mould and play until the book is well worn and all possible avenues have been exhausted.

Whether planning an intimate dinner for two or hosting a dressed-in-full-feather dinner party, I hope you reach for this book, trusting the recipes to deliver on their promise. As always, and without exception, each recipe has been tested more ways than you can shake a stick at. I'd like to believe the margin for error is slimmer than slight. Imagine if they surpass your wildest expectations and tip the scales in favour of home cooking? What a win!

PANTRY & LARDER

The pantry thrives outside of seasonal parameters, making it a dependable source of inspiration year-round. These flavour-boosters shoulder responsibility when the cook is cooked-out and in need of a bright idea or, at the very least, a midweek lifeline.

A well-stocked pantry offers creative short cuts to quick and flavoursome dishes, especially weeknight suppers. Tiered, they look like this:

THE BASIC PANTRY will get you there. No bells and whistles, essentials mostly, but competent, nonetheless.

PREMIUM is a slight upgrade, with the ability to stretch a little further afield.

FIRST CLASS is as you'd expect. Top of the range. You can go anywhere. And go, you should.

There are a couple of tinned basics I am never without – tomatoes, cannellini and butter beans, chickpeas and coconut milk. They're the worker bees. Nothing wild, but capable of doing great things. Raw or tinned, chickpeas are princely staples. Pigeonholing them to hummus would be tragic. We love them roasted, tossed into salads, soups, vegetarian stews and, in our current plant-based favourite, a hearty but very simple Harissa Chickpea Tartine affair (page 97) that's almost a stew, and can pass as brunch or lunch.

Moving on, we have condiments – sweet and savoury preserves, pastes, sauces and nut butters. The larder, or fridge, is where cold things live – dressings, sauces, butters and heat-sensitive preserves. Collectively, these often-overlooked allies come with skill sets that are highly proficient flavour agitators.

TRIVIA: Primitive pantries were used largely to store bread, while a larder was a makeshift – but very clever – cold storage unit fitted with a stone or marble shelf. Food was placed directly on the cool stone, then covered with a flimsy muslin cloth. Not quite a SMEG, but close as damn.

Consol

SUMAC & TAHINI YOGHURT SAUCE

Drizzle over shakshuka, roast vegetables, grain salads, anything along these lines. Thinned out with a splash of water, it leaps from sauce to salad dressing, in which case, maybe add minced garlic, finely chopped chives and flat-leaf parsley.

MAKES 225 ML

125 ml Greek yoghurt
30 ml tahini
45–60 ml water
zest of ½ lemon
15 ml lemon juice
2.5 ml sumac
fine salt and freshly ground black pepper

Place the yoghurt, tahini and water in a small mixing bowl. Whisk until smooth, making sure the tahini is well incorporated.

Add the lemon zest and juice, sumac, salt and black pepper. Whisk together, adding a little more water for a thinner consistency, almost like pouring cream. Transfer to a clean jar, seal and store in the fridge until ready to use. It will keep well for several days.

HARISSA RANCH DRESSING

Light and tangy and great for drizzling over grilled chicken fillets, tacos and burgers. Or, use as a dip with sweet potato wedges. A creamy French-style mayonnaise works best here.

MAKES 200 ML

60 ml buttermilk
60 ml Greek or double-cream plain yoghurt
60 ml mayonnaise
10 ml lemon juice
15 ml harissa paste
1.25 ml each of dried onion powder and garlic powder
fine salt and plenty of freshly ground black pepper

Place all the dressing ingredients in a small bowl and whisk to combine. Taste and adjust the seasoning if needed.

B • V
B • V

CARDAMOM & GIN PLUM JAM

When autumn begins elbowing its way in, just before plums make way for quinces and apples, I haul out the jam pot to make this boozy preserve. You can omit the gin and be no worse off for it, although everyone who tasted it went in for a second spoon. It may be the jam, but then again, it could be the gin. Skimping on the sugar shifts the focus from overly sweet, and settles, rather, on the tangy sourness of the plums. The jelly will be slightly softer, too.

MAKES 3 x 300 ML JARS

- 1 kg plums, rinsed and pitted
- 400–450 g granulated white sugar, according to taste
- 6 cardamom pods, crushed, husks removed, and ground
- 22.5 ml lemon juice
- 125 ml orange juice
- 3 slivers of orange peel
- 1 cinnamon stick
- 5 ml vanilla extract
- 30 ml gin (optional)

Prepare the fruit the night before. Cut the plums into bite-size pieces or slivers. Layer the fruit and sugar in a deep saucepan. Cover and set aside on the counter to macerate overnight.

The next day, place the saucepan over a medium heat. Add the cardamom, lemon juice, orange juice, orange slivers and cinnamon.

Bring slowly up to the boil, stirring gently. Once the sugar is dissolved, turn up the heat and boil hard for 30–35 minutes. Remove from the heat.

Spoon a little jam onto a chilled saucer and place it back in the freezer for 5 minutes. The jam should wrinkle and drag slightly when you run your finger through it.

If you're satisfied with the consistency, stir in the vanilla and gin, if using. Pour the hot jam into sterilized jars and seal immediately.

COOK'S NOTE: Place a saucer in the freezer before starting the jam.

SMOKY AUBERGINE CAPONATA

Chocolate adds a vaguely bitter note, more so than sweetness, to this caponata. Aim for 70% cocoa solids or, better yet, 80%. Serve the caponata with crusty bread and a creamy cheese – burrata, goat's milk cheese or fior di latte.

MAKES 700 ML

- 2 large aubergines, skin on, cut into 2 cm cubes
- olive oil, for roasting and cooking
- fine salt and freshly ground black pepper, to taste
- 2 red onions, finely diced
- 2 long stalks celery, diced
- 1 clove garlic, minced
- 5 ml smoked paprika
- 15 ml tomato paste
- 2.5 ml dried red chilli flakes
- 15 ml brown sugar
- 30 ml balsamic vinegar
- 60 ml red wine vinegar
- 1 x 400 g tin finely chopped tomatoes
- 180 ml water
- 3 squares dark (80%) chocolate
- 40 g sultanas
- 15 ml capers, rinsed
- 30 g pine nuts, toasted
- a handful of fresh basil, roughly chopped

Preheat the oven to 200°C.

Arrange the aubergines in a roasting tin. Drizzle liberally with olive oil and season with salt and black pepper. Roast for 35–40 minutes until golden, tossing halfway through the cooking time. The edges should be nicely charred.

Heat 15 ml olive oil in a deep saucepan. Sauté the onions and celery over a medium heat until softened, about 15 minutes. Stir in the garlic and paprika, and cook for another minute.

Add all the remaining ingredients up to and including the capers. Give the sauce a good stir, then cover and simmer for about 30 minutes. Scrape in the aubergines and add a little more water to loosen the sauce, if needed. Simmer for another 10–15 minutes. Remove from the heat. Add the pine nuts and basil and stir gently to combine.

Divide the hot caponata between sterilized jars. Pour just enough olive oil over the top to cover. Seal and store for up to six weeks in the fridge.

SMOKY CHILLI CRISP

Condiment wild child, chilli crisp can, and does, ruffle feathers. Other than the obvious hangouts – sushi bowls, ramen and Asian-inspired stir-fries – this spicy Asian condiment will perk up your avo toast, scrambled egg and cheese board. Traditionally, chilli crisp has one heat source – chilli flakes. I've added ground guajillo chillies, which are milder, but heavy on smokiness, which I love. You can omit these, though, and still have a very successful crisp. It comes with the obvious, addictive disclaimer.

MAKES 300 ML

250 ml canola or peanut oil
2 shallots, peeled and thinly sliced
3 cloves garlic, thinly sliced
2 dried guajillo chillies, roughly chopped
5 ml Sichuan peppercorns
15–22.5 ml dried red chilli flakes (depending on heat preference)
15 ml grated fresh ginger
60 g roasted salted peanuts, roughly chopped
4 green cardamom pods, crushed
3 star anise
10 ml brown sugar
5 ml Maldon sea salt flakes or to taste
5 ml ground cumin
zest of 1 lemon
15 ml soy sauce

Heat the oil in a small saucepan. Add the shallots and cook over a medium heat until golden, stirring gently to ensure even browning. Remove the shallots with a slotted spoon and drain on paper towel. Add the garlic to the oil and cook as per the shallots. Remove and drain alongside the shallots.

Place the guajillo chillies and Sichuan peppercorns in a processor, and blitz until broken down but not powdery. It should be more flaky, similar to the chilli flakes. Tip into a heatproof bowl. Add the chilli flakes, ginger, peanuts, cardamom pods, star anise, sugar, salt and cumin.

Carefully pour the hot oil (from cooking the shallots and garlic) over the spice mixture. Stir in the lemon zest and soy sauce. Set aside to cool to room temperature.

Once cooled, add the crisp shallots and garlic. Transfer to a clean sterilized jar. Rest overnight to allow the flavours to develop and ripen.

Could keep for several months in the fridge, but won't.

SUNDRIED TOMATO & OLIVE TAPENADE

Some of my best recipes are made in a blender – hummus, dips and pastes for use in appetizers or things destined for cheese boards. A spoon or two, stirred into tomato-based pasta sauces, adds tons of flavour. Pine nuts add a creamy element, moderating the dominant profiles of the olives and sundried tomatoes.

MAKES 350 ML

200 g Kalamata olives, pitted
70 g (8–10) sundried tomatoes
1 red chilli, deseeded and roughly chopped
1.25 ml dried red chilli flakes
1 sprig of rosemary, leaves picked and finely chopped
zest of 1 lemon
10 ml lemon juice
a generous handful each of flat-leaf parsley and basil, leaves picked
30 g pine nuts, toasted
30 ml extra virgin olive oil, plus extra to drizzle
freshly ground black pepper

Place the olives and sundried tomatoes in a processor and pulse until broken down. Add the chopped chilli, dried chilli flakes, rosemary and lemon zest. Blitz at 20-second intervals until the desired texture is reached.

Add the remaining ingredients and pulse briefly to combine. Scrape into a sterilized jar and pour over a thin film of olive oil. Seal and store in the fridge for up to two weeks.

COOK'S NOTE: *Always serve at room temperature.*

SPECULAAS NUT BUTTER

I still remember the day a primary school classmate returned from a holiday in Amsterdam. He brought everyone a tiny packet of *stroopwafels*, those famed Dutch cookies glued together with caramel. The flavourings of this nut butter are a mishmash of classic Dutch cookie flavourings – cinnamon spice and all things nice.

This nut butter can be spread on toast, drizzled over oats, in smoothies or sandwiched between cookies. Failing that, grab a spoon ...

MAKES 300 ML

- 300 g raw mixed nuts (almonds, cashews, macadamia and pecans)
- 5 ml ground cinnamon
- 2.5 ml ground mixed spice
- a generous pinch of ground nutmeg
- 1.25 ml Maldon sea salt flakes
- 30 ml maple syrup or honey
- 10 ml coconut oil, melted

Preheat the oven to 180°C.

Spread the nuts onto a baking sheet and roast for 10–12 minutes, turning them over halfway to ensure even browning. Set aside to cool.

Transfer the nuts to a high-speed blender. Pulse at 30-second intervals until broken down. The texture will look somewhat rubble-like at first. Scrape down the sides, then continue blending until the consistency is smooth and silky.

Add the spices, salt, maple syrup or honey, and coconut oil. Blend at intervals until the nut butter turns glossy and smooth once more. Transfer to a sterilized jar and seal.

COOK'S NOTES: Homemade nut butters can be stored for up to six weeks in the pantry or three months in the fridge.

Roasting nuts before grinding them into a paste accentuates their nuttiness.

TOASTY SEED SPRINKLES

There are some recipes I make on repeat. This is one of them. What are sprinkles good for? Just about anything, really. Salads, soup toppings, avocado toast, salads and salty snacks.

MAKES 280 G

70 g sunflower seeds
75 g pumpkin seeds
40 g pine nuts
30 g white sesame seeds
10 g black sesame seeds
2.5 ml dried oregano
5 ml smoked paprika
5 ml ground cumin
zest of 1 small lemon
1.25 ml Maldon sea salt flakes
freshly ground black pepper
12.5 ml extra virgin olive oil
15 ml soy sauce

Place the sunflower seeds, pumpkin seeds and pine nuts in a wide-based pan. Toast over a medium heat until golden, stirring from time to time to keep the pine nuts from catching. Scrape onto a plate.

In the same pan, toast the white and black sesame seeds for 2–3 minutes. Add the sunflower seeds, pumpkin seeds and pine nuts back into the pan.

Season with oregano, paprika, cumin, lemon zest, salt and black pepper. Place over a low heat to bloom the spices, a minute or two at most.

Drizzle over the olive oil and soy sauce, stirring quickly to coat the seeds. Set aside to cool before storing in an airtight container.

TAHINI CAESAR DRESSING

Tahini has many talents, but none so impressive as the ease with which it adapts to sweet or savoury combinations. Besides the obvious nuttiness, its bitter edge and rich toasty notes add creamy appeal to dressings and sauces.

Drizzle over leafy greens, a classic Caesar salad and autumnal roast veg. Replace the nutritional yeast with parmesan and the maple syrup with honey, if you're not needing it to be vegan.

MAKES 250 ML

- 60 ml tahini
- 1 clove garlic
- 5 ml Dijon mustard
- 10 ml maple syrup
- a pinch of cayenne pepper
- zest of 1 lemon
- 37.5 ml lemon juice
- 30 ml nutritional yeast
- 45 ml extra virgin olive oil
- 100 ml water
- 3.75 ml Maldon sea salt flakes
- freshly ground black pepper

Place all the ingredients in a blender and blitz until smooth. It will keep for several days, chilled.

VINAIGRETTES

A salad is just a bunch of greens until properly dressed. That's where hard-hitting vinaigrettes and dressings save the day. Once the ratio of oil and acid is balanced, it can go in any direction. Finely chopped herbs, shallots, minced garlic and ground spices are great flavour activists. When making a wintery pear salad, for example, I swap the olive oil for hazelnut or walnut oil.

CLASSIC VINAIGRETTE

MAKES 120 ML

- 60 ml extra virgin olive oil
- 15 ml prosecco vinegar or apple cider vinegar
- 30 ml fresh lemon juice
- zest of ½ lemon
- 5 ml Dijon mustard
- 5 ml honey or maple syrup
- 3.75 ml Maldon sea salt flakes and a few twists of freshly ground black pepper

ORANGE & CORIANDER VINAIGRETTE

MAKES 145 ML

- 60 ml extra virgin olive oil
- 15 ml apple cider vinegar
- 30 ml fresh lemon juice
- 30 ml orange juice
- zest of 1 orange
- 5 ml ground coriander
- 7.5 ml Dijon mustard
- 10 ml honey or maple syrup
- 3.75 ml Maldon sea salt flakes
- freshly ground black pepper

ZA'ATAR & MINT VINAIGRETTE

MAKES 140 ML

- 60 ml extra virgin olive oil
- 45 ml fresh lemon juice
- 3.75 ml sumac
- 5 ml dried mint
- 30 ml za'atar
- 10 ml pomegranate syrup or honey
- 3.75 ml Maldon sea salt flakes and freshly ground black pepper

Place all the ingredients in a lidded jar and shake vigorously. Taste and adjust seasoning according to taste.

SALTED BUTTER

My Ouma Martha could make just about anything. I remember watching her make butter. Using freshly skimmed cream, she would churn that wooden paddle mercilessly until buttery droplets clustered together, the milky white liquid sloshing up against the sides. It required a fair bit of elbow grease, of which she lacked none. Spread thickly on her just-baked boerebrood, it was indeed the exquisiteness of simple.

MAKES 380 G

750 ml double thick cream, chilled
1.25 ml fine salt

Place the cream in the bowl of a free-standing mixer with the balloon whisk attachment.

Starting on a medium speed, whisk until the cream thickens slightly. Scrape down the sides of the bowl, then cover the mixer loosely with a clean tea towel to prevent splashing. Turn the speed to high and whisk until the buttermilk separates from the butter, 3–4 minutes should suffice.

Strain the mixture (reserving the buttermilk to use for pancakes or scones) through a sieve or fine colander. Press the butter together to force out as much liquid as possible.

Fill a clean bowl with ice water and rinse the butter several times in clean water, each time pressing together to expel any residual buttermilk. This will ensure the butter stays fresher for longer. Add the salt and work it through the butter, then wrap in greaseproof paper and chill until firm.

COOK'S NOTE: Below I've included several flavoured butters. Each one yields 125 g.

MISO & BLACK SESAME SEED BUTTER

125 g butter
10 ml white miso paste
15 ml black sesame seeds, toasted

ROAST GARLIC, HERB & PARMESAN BUTTER

125 g butter
1 clove garlic, roasted
25 g chopped mixed fresh herbs (flat-leaf parsley, rosemary, thyme, basil)
60 ml grated parmesan
15 ml extra virgin olive oil
freshly ground black pepper

MARMITE & BLACK PEPPER BUTTER

125 g butter
15 ml Marmite
1.25 ml freshly ground black pepper

FOR THE FLAVOURED BUTTERS, combine 125 g softened butter with your choice of flavourings. Scrape onto a sheet of baking paper. Roll into a cylinder, twisting the ends to close. Chill until firm.

LIME CURD

Bottled in recycled Rose's Marmalade jars, Granny Cora's lemon curd was first-rate. On holidays, we'd gather in my grandparents' cramped, but cheerful, breakfast room, diagonally across from the kitchen, with hot buttered toast and her famous curd. This is my quick version, made with limes.

MAKES ABOUT 350 ML

220 g granulated white sugar
80 ml lime juice (3–4 limes)
zest of 1 lime
2 whole eggs, plus 1 egg yolk
80 g butter, cut into cubes
a pinch of fine salt

Place the sugar, lime juice and zest in a heatproof bowl and whisk to combine. Add the eggs and egg yolk, and whisk well to combine.

Microwave on high for 1 minute. Whisk thoroughly, then repeat the process three more times, whisking well each time to bring the temperature down and ensure even cooking.

Add the butter and salt, whisking well until smooth and glossy. Strain the curd before pouring into a sterilized jar. Seal and store in the fridge once cooled.

COOK'S NOTE: A bright yellow colour denotes a high ratio of eggs. Curd will keep well in a sterilized jar in the fridge for 3–4 weeks. Apparently, it can be frozen, although I can't vouch for this. Nothing in my fridge experiences the privilege of old age.

TRIVIA: Lemon curd became a fashionable replacement for jam back in the 19th century. It was used to fill cakes, pastries and tarts. Gracing afternoon tea tables as a topping for scones and cream, it is now commonplace as a preserve alternative.

PRESERVED LEMON – IN A HURRY! Wash 2 medium lemons in hot water to remove the waxiness on the skin. Cut into quarters. Add to a small saucepan with 250 ml water, 15 ml Maldon sea salt flakes and 10 ml sugar. Bring to a boil, then simmer on medium-low for 60 minutes. Transfer to a sterilized jar and stand at room temperature overnight. Store chilled for up to three weeks.

GODDESS AVOCADO DRESSING

A green goddess is lively and fresh. Typically, it combines heaps of soft-leaf herbs and, oftentimes, spinach, with a tangy base of yoghurt and lemon. I've added tahini for a nutty nuance, and creamy superfood, avocado. It keeps well in the fridge for several days. Covering the top of the dressing with a little cold water will help prevent discolouration.

MAKES 300 ML

1 small avocado
60 ml Greek yoghurt
30 ml tahini
50 g loosely packed mixed fresh herbs (parsley, coriander, mint, rocket)
1 clove garlic
30 ml lemon juice
45 ml extra virgin olive oil
80 ml cold water
Maldon sea salt flakes and freshly ground black pepper, to taste

Place all the ingredients in a high-speed blender and blitz until smooth. Drizzle in a splash of cold water to thin down the sauce, if you're using it as a salad dressing. For burgers, a slightly thicker consistency is best.

DATE SYRUP

If you're a DIY cook or just plain curious, this project is for you. Date syrup is a competent sugar replacement, on par with honey or maple syrup. Use it in place of refined sugars in baked goods – muffins, banana bread and the like, or drizzle over pancakes and yoghurt. I usually double the quantity, in which case increase the cooking time by 8–10 minutes.

MAKES 200–220 ML

500 g pitted Medjool dates

Roughly chop the dates, then place in a large heatproof bowl. Cover with boiling water, just enough to submerge the dates. Set aside to soak for 60 minutes.

Transfer the softened dates and soaking water to a deep saucepan. Add 1.25 litres of hot water. Bring slowly up to the boil, then reduce the heat and simmer over a medium heat for 30 minutes. Roughly mash the dates with the back of a wooden spoon or potato masher, cover partially and simmer for a further 30 minutes. Set aside until cool to the touch.

Line a sieve or large strainer with a muslin cloth set over a deep bowl. Working in batches, tip a third of the cooled pulp into the cloth. Twist firmly to remove as much liquid as possible. Discard the dry pulp and repeat with the remaining date mixture. You should end up with close to 1 litre of strained liquid.

Pour the date liquid back into the saucepan and bring it up to a rolling boil. Boil until the liquid is reduced and syrupy – 20–30 minutes, depending on the size of the saucepan and strength of the heat source. The wider the base, the faster the reducing time.

BUTTER CHICKEN CURRY PASTE

When it comes to curries, toasting whole spices goes a long way to emphasizing their concealed potential. It's worth the extra step. Adding cashews is neither authentic nor essential, but I'm prepared to run the gauntlet in pursuit of deliciousness.

MAKES 320 ML (USE ± 160 ML PER RECIPE FOR BUTTER CHICKEN)

- 40 g raw unsalted cashew nuts
- 22.5 ml cumin seeds
- 15 ml coriander seeds
- 5 whole cloves
- 1 star anise, crushed
- 1 cinnamon stick
- 6 cardamom pods, crushed, husks discarded
- 2 large red onions, diced
- vegetable oil, for cooking plus extra for covering
- 3–4 cloves garlic, minced
- 45 ml grated fresh ginger
- 22.5 ml garam masala
- 15 ml dried red chilli flakes
- 5 ml chilli powder
- 15 ml paprika
- 10 ml Maldon sea salt flakes
- 10 ml brown sugar
- 50 g tomato paste
- 250 ml water

Place the cashews in a bowl and cover with boiling water. Set aside to soften, around 20 minutes.

Dry-toast the cumin, coriander, cloves, star anise and cinnamon stick in a pan until fragrant, 3–4 minutes. Transfer to a spice grinder, along with the cardamom pods, and pulse until finely ground.

Sauté the onions in 30 ml oil over a medium-low heat until softened and caramelized, about 20 minutes. Stir in the garlic and ginger, and cook for 2 minutes. Add the freshly ground spices, garam masala, chilli flakes, chilli powder, paprika, salt and sugar. Give the onions a good mix, coating them in the spices.

Drain the cashews, then add to the onions along with the tomato paste and water. Simmer over a low heat for 10 minutes.

Transfer the mixture to a processor. Add 15 ml oil and blitz until smooth. Spoon into a sterilized jar. Drizzle a little vegetable oil over the top, just enough to cover the paste, then seal and store in the fridge for up to three weeks.

BUTTER CHICKEN CURRY PASTE IDEAS

Butter chicken rotis, Roast butternut and chickpea curry, Chicken burgers, Butter chicken meatballs in coconut cream.

FLOUR
SALT
WATER
YEAST

– BREAD –

Bread is one of the simplest yet most delicious depictions of culture. Woven into its floury genes are centuries-old stories of sustenance, community and historic relevance.

Whether simply shaped or embellished with dried fruits and spices, bread remains the ceremonious opener that welcomes guests at the table. Is there anything that weakens resolve and warms the heart like bread and butter?

Good bread is as much about the quality of the flour as it is about patience. Anyone who knows their bread will tell you that the secret ingredient is nothing more than intuition. Is it thirsty or over-watered, too dimpled, not dimpled enough or just highly strung? The clues are everywhere. It helps tremendously if you're a bread whisperer. But, once you've cracked the code, the journey from flour to staff of life is as nurturing and restorative as it is artistically rewarding.

Slow overnight proofing in a cold environment (the fridge), encourages stable gluten structure and kindles a well-rounded flavour, so I often opt for this method. Instant or fast-action yeasted breads become unpleasantly sour if left too long. A day, two at most, is ample proofing time. Enriched doughs, with added fats, either butter or oil, eggs and milk, retard the proofing process, so bear this in mind when baking sweetened breads.

For all breads, allow 15–30 g flour for correcting the consistency. Use only if needed, after the initial liquid is added to the dry ingredients and the dough still appears a little too wet.

WHEAT FLOUR SUBSTITUTES

The elasticity of gluten in wheat flour is what gives bread its distinguishable chewy crumb. However, there are tons of wheat-free alternatives that, when combined correctly, yield the desired results.

Wheat-free flour options include buckwheat, certified gluten-free oat flour, coconut flour, tapioca flour, cassava flour, rice flour, nut flours and flaxseed meal.

HOKKAIDO – JAPANESE MILK BREAD

It sounds more complicated than it is, although the concept is nothing short of genius. Our starter dough, pronounced 'tang-zong', refers to the science of incorporating additional moisture without necessarily adding more liquid.

Ethereally light, like whimsical strands that melt in the mouth.

MAKES 1 LOAF

TANGZHONG (STARTER)
30 g white bread flour
60 ml water, room temperature
60 ml full-cream milk

DOUGH
125 ml full-cream milk, tepid temperature
10 ml (7 g) instant dry yeast
1 egg
60 ml buttermilk
360 g white bread flour, plus 15–30 g for correcting
5 ml fine salt
45 ml castor sugar
50 g butter, softened

egg wash (1 egg whisked with 15 ml milk)

START BY MAKING THE TANGZHONG. In a small saucepan, combine the flour and water. Whisk to ensure the mixture is free of lumps. Add the milk and mix to combine. Cook for several minutes, as you would a roux, until the mixture forms a thick paste. Remove to a small dish, cover and set aside to cool.

TO MAKE THE DOUGH, whisk the milk and yeast together in a jug. Set aside for 10 minutes. Add the egg and buttermilk, and whisk to combine.

Place the flour, salt and castor sugar in the bowl of an electric mixer fitted with the dough hook attachment. Add the milk mixture and tangzhong, and mix to combine. Knead on a low speed for 5–6 minutes. Add the butter, 1 tablespoon at a time. Knead for several minutes until all the butter is incorporated and the dough is smooth.

Place the dough in an oiled bowl and set aside to proof for 2–2½ hours, or until doubled in size. Alternatively, proof in the fridge overnight. Bring to room temperature before continuing.

Butter and line a 26 x 12 cm loaf tin with baking paper. Preheat the oven to 180°C.

Turn out the dough onto a lightly floured surface. Divide into five equal pieces. Cover and rest for 20 minutes. This resting period will prevent the dough from springing back when rolling.

Roll each piece into a rough square of about 18 cm. Turn the dough at an angle to form a kite shape. Fold the left, then the right, points towards the centre, then fold the top down to meet at the centre. Roll up gently from the bottom. Place in the loaf tin, seam side down. Repeat with the remaining pieces, placing them side by side down the length of the tin.

Cover and set aside to proof until doubled in size, 45–60 minutes.

Brush with egg wash and bake for 35–40 minutes. Cover with foil for the last 10 minutes of the baking time, if the top is browning too rapidly.

Cool in the tin for 10 minutes before turning out onto a wire rack to cool completely.

DANISH OAT & HONEY WHOLEMEAL LOAF

Only recently did I discover the genius of toasted milk powder. Mixing it into cookies, cakes or, in this instance, bread, adds milk fat solids without disrupting the delicate wet to dry ratio. The result is an enriched bake, imbued with browned caramel undertones. I make a large batch and keep it on hand for bake days. Although, you can leave it out and still have a perfectly good loaf, if you're just not into toasting stuff. The focus is, after all, on the oats.

MAKES 1 x 20 CM ROUND LOAF

- 250 ml low-fat milk, plus 15 ml extra for brushing
- 125 ml water
- 20 g toasted milk powder (*see instructions below*)
- 45 ml butter
- 30 ml honey
- 90 g whole rolled oats, plus extra for topping
- 225 g stoneground white bread flour
- 150 g stoneground wholemeal flour
- 35 g rye flour
- 5 ml fine salt
- 10 ml (7 g) instant dry yeast

Place the milk, water, toasted milk powder, butter and honey in a small saucepan. Heat until the butter is melted. Add the oats and stir to combine. Remove from the heat and set aside to cool.

Add the white bread flour, wholemeal flour, rye flour, salt and yeast to the bowl of a stand mixer. Whisk briefly to combine.

Once the milk mixture is at room temperature, add it to the dry ingredients. With the dough hook attachment, mix on a medium-low speed to combine, then knead for 6–8 minutes.

Scrape the dough into a lightly oiled bowl, cover and set aside to proof until doubled in size, 60–90 minutes.

Butter and line a 20 cm round cake tin with baking paper.

Turn the dough out onto a lightly floured surface. Knock down, then shape into a 20 cm round. Place the dough in the tin, cover with a tea towel and set aside to proof until doubled in size.

Preheat the oven to 180°C.

Brush the top of the dough with milk and scatter over a handful of oats. Bake for 40–45 minutes, or until golden and cooked through. Cool on a wire rack before slicing.

COOK'S NOTE: The method for softening the oats in milk is adapted from The Great Scandinavian Baking Book *by Beatrice Ojakangas.*

TOASTED MILK POWDER Place the powdered milk in a dry, non-stick pan. Cook over a gentle heat, stirring constantly until deeply golden, 5–6 minutes. Cool before storing.

WHOLEMEAL PITA BREAD

I can't think of one good reason why not to make your own pitas. The bake time is under 4 minutes, almost instant in bread years.

MAKES 8

- 300 ml water, tepid temperature
- 5 ml castor sugar
- 10 ml (7 g) instant dry yeast
- 120 g wholegrain spelt flour or fine wholemeal flour
- 30 ml olive oil
- 300 g stoneground white bread flour
- 6.25 ml fine salt

In the bowl of a stand mixer, combine the water, sugar and yeast. Add 50 g of the wholegrain flour and whisk to combine. Set aside for 15–20 minutes until foamy.

Add the oil to the yeast mixture, followed by the remaining wholegrain flour, bread flour and salt. With the dough hook attachment, mix on a low speed to combine. Knead for 6–8 minutes until the dough is smooth and supple. Transfer to an oiled bowl, cover with a tea towel and set aside to proof until doubled in size, 45–60 minutes.

Preheat the oven to 250°C. Place a baking sheet in the oven – the middle rack – while the oven heats.

Divide the dough into eight equal portions. Roll into balls, then cover with a tea towel and rest for 15 minutes.

On a floured surface, roll out each ball into a 15 cm diameter circle, about 3 mm thick. Place four rounds onto the heated baking sheet. Bake for 4 minutes until puffed and golden. Repeat with the second batch.

Wrap loosely in a large tea towel to keep warm.

EASY FLATBREADS

Ready to do the work of a spoon. Perfect hummus and dip scoopers, anything mezze-like, or fill with fresh salad and hot-off-the-grid kebabs.

MAKES 6

200 g cake wheat flour
150 g wholegrain spelt flour or stoneground wholemeal flour
3.75 ml baking powder
5 ml fine salt
125 ml water
125 ml full-cream milk
30 ml extra virgin olive oil
vegetable oil, for cooking

Sift the cake wheat flour, wholegrain flour, baking powder and salt into a mixing bowl.

Place the water, milk and olive oil in a small jug, and whisk to combine. Add the liquid to the dry ingredients. Using a fork, mix until the dough clumps together.

Turn out onto a lightly floured surface and knead for 2–3 minutes. Place in an oiled bowl, cover and set aside to rest for 30 minutes.

Divide the dough into six equal portions. Dust the countertop with flour. Roll each portion into 20 cm rounds, 2–3 mm thick.

Heat a non-stick pan until hot, then brush lightly with vegetable oil. Lay the flatbread in the pan and cook until puffed, with dark brown patches underneath. Turn and cook the other side for another minute or so. Repeat with the remaining flatbreads.

Wrap in a tea towel to keep warm. Layering one atop another and wrapping in a cloth will yield a softer, more 'flexible' flatbread.

OLIVE OIL & ROSEMARY BUCKWHEAT CRACKERS

When friends pop by unexpectedly, having a stash of these savoury crackerbreads on hand can save the day. Offer with hummus, dips, cheese, maybe figs or quince jelly – fridge door things – and a lovely, chilled chenin.

You'll need to roll the dough quite thinly to ensure a crisp, dry texture. Once cool, snap into shards.

MAKES 6 LARGE SHARDS

140 g cake wheat flour
100 g wholegrain spelt flour
70 g buckwheat flour
3.75 ml fine salt
1.25 ml freshly ground black pepper
15 ml finely chopped fresh rosemary
3.75 ml dried thyme
50 g sesame seeds
40 g sunflower seeds
160 ml water
80 ml olive oil
egg wash, to finish (1 egg whisked with 15 ml water)
Maldon sea salt flakes and freshly ground black pepper, to finish

Preheat the oven to 180°C. Line a large baking sheet with baking paper.

In a mixing bowl, combine all three flours, salt, black pepper, rosemary, thyme, sesame seeds and sunflower seeds. Add the water and olive oil. Using a fork, mix until the dough forms a scraggly mass. Turn out onto a floured surface and knead for several minutes.

Wrap in cling film and chill for at least 30 minutes, or overnight if you only want to bake these the following day.

Divide the dough into six equal pieces. On a lightly floured surface, roll out into a sort of slipper shape, 2 mm thick. Transfer to the baking sheet.

Brush the tops lightly with egg wash. Scatter over a little sea salt flakes and a generous grinding of black pepper. Bake for 22–24 minutes, rotating the baking sheet after 15 minutes.

Cool completely before storing in an airtight container.

COOK'S NOTE: *I manage to fit 3–4 pieces of dough on a large baking sheet, so bake in batches.*

VENETIAN PIZZA TILES

If you like pizza, you're going to love these Italian-inspired crackers. They need nothing on the side or on top. Straight up deliciousness. Pre-dinner drinks or cocktail ready. Like peanuts and popcorn – unstoppable once you start.

MAKES ROUGHLY 70

1 x full quantity prepared poolish (*see* below) or 260 g sourdough discard
45 ml olive oil
75 g cake wheat flour
75 g wholegrain spelt flour
2.5 ml fine salt
1.25 ml freshly ground black pepper
1 sprig of fresh rosemary, leaves picked and finely chopped
5 ml herbes de Provence
2.5 ml paprika
1.25 ml dried red chilli flakes
1.25 ml dried garlic flakes
25 g parmesan, finely grated
40 g mixed seeds (pumpkin, sunflower, sesame, flaxseed)
egg wash (1 egg whisked with 15 ml water)
Maldon sea salt flakes and freshly ground black pepper, to finish

Scrape the poolish into a large mixing bowl. Add the olive oil and mix well to combine.

Add all the remaining ingredients, up to and including the mixed seeds. Using a wooden spoon, mix everything together, scraping any dry bits at the bottom of the bowl into the dough. Tip onto the counter and knead lightly until the dough comes together. Place in an oiled bowl, cover and set aside to rest for 1 hour.

Preheat the oven to 180°C.

On a lightly floured surface, roll out the dough into a rectangle, around 3 mm thick. Transfer carefully onto a sheet of baking paper. Cut the dough into 3 cm diagonal shapes, then slide the paper onto a large baking sheet.

Brush the top with egg wash and scatter lightly with sea salt flakes and black pepper. Bake for 22–24 minutes, rotating the baking sheet after 15 minutes.

Once cooled, snap into tiles and store in an airtight container.

POOLISH Combine a generous pinch of instant dry yeast with 180 ml water. Add 125 g stoneground white bread flour and mix into a homogenous batter. Cover and place on the counter for 12–16 hours.

SWEDISH CARDAMOM BUNS

If I had to choose just one bakery bun, it would be these Swedish knots. One buttery twist and you'll be down the rabbit hole. Admittedly, they're a fair bit of work, but cheaper than a ticket to Stockholm.

MAKES 12–14

DOUGH
380 g cake wheat flour
3.75 ml fine salt
45 g castor sugar
200 ml fullcream milk, slightly warmed
10 ml (7 g) instant dry yeast
60 g butter, melted and cooled
1 egg
egg wash (1 egg whisked with 15 ml water)
pearled sugar to finish (optional)

FILLING
80 g butter, softened
70 g soft brown sugar
10 ml ground cinnamon
2.5 ml ground mixed spice
5 ml ground cardamom

CARDAMOM SYRUP
45 ml water
45 ml castor sugar
5 cardamom pods, crushed
2.5 ml vanilla paste

FOR THE DOUGH, place the flour, salt and sugar in the bowl of an electric mixer fitted with the dough hook attachment. Mix briefly to combine.

In a jug, whisk together the milk and yeast. Set aside for 10 minutes.

Whisk the butter and egg together. Add to the flour, along with the milk mixture. Mix on a low speed until the dough is smooth and pliable, about 8 minutes. Transfer to a lightly oiled bowl, cover and set aside to proof until doubled in size, about 2 hours.

TO MAKE THE FILLING, combine the butter, sugar and spices to form a smooth paste.

Turn the dough out onto a lightly floured surface. Roll into a square, roughly 40 x 40 cm. Spread the filling over the entire surface. Fold into thirds, as you would a business letter, then roll into a rectangle measuring 35 x 22 cm. Trim the edges to neaten.

With the length of the dough running horizontally, cut into lengths, each measuring 2.5 cm in width. Now cut each strip in half, keeping 1 cm attached at the top. Twist the dough gently, then wrap twice around three fingers, then over the top, securing the ends underneath. Arrange on a lined baking sheet. Cover and set aside to proof until doubled in size once more, 45–60 minutes.

FOR THE CARDAMOM SYRUP, combine all the ingredients in a saucepan. Boil for 3 minutes, then strain.

Preheat the oven to 180°C.

Brush the buns with egg wash and scatter over the pearled sugar, if using. Bake for 25 minutes. As soon as the buns come out of the oven, brush them liberally with the cardamom syrup.

SIX-STRAND CHALLAH

Honey and olive oil drive this challah into new territories. The difference is subtle, yet lively and modern. Once you fall into the plaiting rhythm, you are halfway there. A simpler three-strand is just as good, but I love the taste of 'concentrated effort', so a six-strand it shall be. Leftover challah makes the best French toast and bread pudding. Eat one, repurpose the other.

MAKES 2

- 425 ml water, tepid temperature
- 12.5 ml (10 g) instant dry yeast
- 30 ml honey
- 3 eggs
- 60 ml extra virgin olive oil
- 60 ml vegetable oil
- 1 kg cake wheat flour, plus 15–30 g for correcting
- 12.5 ml fine salt
- 70 g castor sugar
- egg wash (1 egg whisked with 15 ml water)

Combine the water, yeast and honey in a mixing bowl, whisking to dissolve the honey. Set aside until foamy, about 10 minutes. Add the eggs, olive oil and vegetable oil. Whisk to combine.

Add the flour, salt and castor sugar to the bowl of an electric mixer fitted with the dough hook attachment. Mix on low speed to combine. Add the yeast mixture to the flour and mix to combine. Knead for 6–8 minutes until smooth and elastic. Place the dough in a large, oiled bowl, cover with cling film and set aside to proof until doubled in size, about 1 hour, more if it's cold.

Turn out the dough onto a lightly floured surface. Halve the dough to make two loaves.

Divide each portion into six smaller balls. Cover with a tea towel and rest for 20 minutes.

Roll out each ball into a long strand measuring 40–45 cm in length. Place six strands alongside each other with a 1.5 cm spacing. Pinch the top ends together.

Start with the strand that is furthest right. Lift and cross it over to the left. Now, take the strand that had initially been on the far left and cross it over to the far right. Lift the strand that is now on the left side and place it down the centre. Try to keep a middle path clear throughout the braiding. Lift the strand second to the right and cross it over and up towards the left. Place the strand on the right down the middle. Repeat the same pattern to the end. Pinch the ends firmly together and tuck underneath to neaten.

Repeat the process with the remaining dough.

Lift carefully and place on a large, lined baking sheet, allowing room for spreading. Cover with a clean tea towel and set aside to proof until doubled in size.

Preheat the oven to 180°C.

Brush the challah with egg wash, making sure to cover all the nooks and crannies. Keep any remaining egg wash aside for later.

Bake for 27–30 minutes. Remove the bread from the oven and brush the paler crevices with more egg wash. Bake for a further 8 minutes. Cool before slicing.

CINNAMON & CARDAMOM PULL-APART BREAD WITH BOURBON GLAZE

The baking playground is strewn with delicious knick-knacks that add character and textural interest. It's really a case of use what you prefer or have on hand – dried fruit, nuts and sweet spices – cinnamon, cardamom and the extended family. Nutella does a fine job, too, if chocolate is more up your alley.

Stacking the dough squares, one atop the other, before nestling in a loaf tin, turns bread on its head. Irregularity is part of the charm, so don't bother with perfection.

MAKES 1 LOAF

DOUGH
380 g cake wheat flour, plus 15–30 g for correcting
10 ml (7 g) instant dry yeast
50 g castor sugar
2.5 ml fine salt
80 ml full-cream milk, tepid temperature
60 ml water, tepid temperature
60 g butter, melted
2 eggs, room temperature

SPICED BUTTER
50 g butter, room temperature
60 g brown sugar
12.5 ml ground cinnamon
2.5 ml ground mixed spice
6 cardamom pods, crushed, husks removed, and finely ground
a pinch of fine salt

BOURBON GLAZE
125 g cream cheese, room temperature
60 g butter, softened
5 ml vanilla extract
22.5 ml bourbon (optional)
130 g icing sugar, sifted
a pinch of fine salt

TO MAKE THE DOUGH, place the flour, yeast, sugar and salt in the bowl of a stand mixer fitted with the dough hook attachment. In a jug, whisk together the milk, water, melted butter and eggs. Add the wet ingredients to the dry and mix to combine. Knead until smooth and elastic, 6–8 minutes. Transfer to an oiled bowl, cover and set aside until doubled in size.

Butter and line a 22 x 12 cm loaf tin.

Turn the dough out onto a lightly floured surface. Roll out to measure 48 x 32 cm. Neaten the edges using a pizza cutter or smooth-bladed knife.

FOR THE SPICED BUTTER, combine the butter, sugar, spices and salt. Spread the butter evenly over the dough. Working from the long side, cut the dough into six lengths, each with a width of 8 cm. Cut each strip into quarters. In total, you should have 24 squares. Stack four squares on top of each other, turn them sideways and stack them into the loaf tin, cut side down. Continue with the remaining squares. Cover and set aside to proof for 45–60 minutes.

Preheat the oven to 180°C. Bake for 40 minutes until golden and cooked through. Cover loosely with foil for the last 10 minutes of the baking time. Rest in the tin for 20 minutes before removing to a cooling rack.

FOR THE GLAZE, whisk the cream cheese until smooth. Add the butter, vanilla and bourbon, if using, and whisk until smooth. Sift in the icing sugar and salt, and whisk to combine. Spread half the glaze over the bread whilst warm, serving the remainder alongside.

SEED & NUT OAT BREAD

The pre-bake resting period helps soften and swell the oats and chia seeds. Fresh or toasted, this bread makes an excellent carrier for sweet or savoury toppings. It freezes well too, which is helpful if you're not feeding the five thousand. Slice before freezing, then defrost and toast as needed.

MAKES 1 x 22 CM LOAF

225 g whole rolled oats
270 g mixed seeds (120 g each of sunflower and pumpkin seeds, 30 g sesame seeds)
50 g almonds, roughly chopped
20 g psyllium husk
35 g chia seeds
25 g flaxseed meal
7.5 ml Maldon sea salt flakes
400 ml water, tepid temperature
15 ml honey
15 ml olive oil

Line a 22 x 10 cm loaf tin with baking paper, allowing the paper to extend over the sides, creating handles, for lifting the bread out of the tin.

Place all the dry ingredients, up to and including the salt, in a large bowl. Mix to combine.

In a jug, whisk together the water, honey and oil. Add the liquid to the dry ingredients and mix to form a softish, wet dough. Cover and set aside for 45 minutes.

Preheat the oven to 180°C.

Scrape the mixture into the tin and press down firmly. Bake for 55 minutes. Remove the loaf from the tin. Invert onto an oven rack, remove the baking paper and bake for an additional 10 minutes.

Cool completely before slicing.

COOK'S NOTE: Slice thinly and toast before adding to a cheese board.

OVERNIGHT FOCACCIA

The bubble activity is wildly exciting. So too is opening the oven door to a gust of Italian air that smells of rosemary, olives and browned butter. Expect nothing less than a bronzed crust that's audibly crisp. Once baked, wait as long as you think is appropriate. Two minutes sound about right?

SERVES 10–12

350 g stoneground white bread flour
150 g Tipo 00 flour
5 ml fine salt
500 ml water, tepid temperature
10 ml (7 g) instant dry yeast
5 ml castor sugar
45 ml extra virgin olive oil, plus extra to drizzle
30 ml melted butter to finish, plus extra for greasing

SALAMOIA
30 ml extra virgin olive oil
30 ml water, room temperature
2–3 sprigs of fresh rosemary, leaves picked
Maldon sea salt flakes

Sift the bread flour, Tipo 00 flour and salt together in a large mixing bowl.

Place the water, yeast and sugar in a jug and whisk together. Set aside for 10 minutes until creamy.

Whisk 15 ml olive oil into the yeast mixture, then add it to the dry ingredients. Mix well to incorporate all the flour until there are no visible dry spots. Drizzle 15 ml olive oil into a large mixing bowl. Scrape in the dough, then turn gently to coat in the oil. Cover and chill overnight. Bring the dough to room temperature before continuing.

Using a fork and working from the outer edges, scrape the dough upwards and over towards the centre. Turn the bowl slightly, then repeat the lift and fold action in increments of eight to complete a full circle. Cover and rest for 1 hour.

Butter the base and sides of a 35 x 22 cm roasting tin with butter. Drizzle over 15 ml olive oil, spreading it over the butter. With wet hands, scrape the dough into the roasting tin, stretching it gently into the corners. Cover with a tea towel and place in a warm spot to proof until doubled in size, 2–3 hours.

Preheat the oven to 230°C.

FOR THE SALAMOIA, whisk the oil and water together. Add the rosemary and stir through. Dimple the dough lightly with your fingertips. Pour the salamoia over the surface and scatter with sea salt flakes. Bake for 30–35 minutes, covering the top with foil for the last 5–10 minutes if it darkens too quickly. Transfer to a wire rack to cool slightly. Brush with melted butter just before serving.

MORNING GLOW

–SWEET & SAVOURY–

There's only one thing better than breakfast – brunch.

An hour or two spent preparing for the week ahead goes a long way to making busy weekday mornings less stressful, and most certainly more delicious. Regulars at our breakfast table are smoothies, granola – with berries and yoghurt – and, on a good day, maybe a batch of waffles or crêpes. But, before we even get to the table, it's rusks and coffee in bed. Yes, another rusk recipe (page 78), although this one is refined sugar-free, with coconut sugar and honey helping it hit the bliss point. The Banana & Apple Muffin Loaf with Cinnamon Streusel on page 84 is more breakfast than it is cake (baked on a Sunday) and brimming with good-for-you ingredients. Tender and warmly spiced with pockets of juicy apples. We love it warm, with thick yoghurt and a drizzle of honey.

If there is one brunch recipe you should stick a Post-it on, it's the Summer Berry Brunch Crumble (page 88). The girls and I have made it for wellness events, breakfast and dessert. There's been nothing but wild swooning over it and requests for the recipe. I think you're going to love it, too.

Savoury breakfasts are a little trickier, often needing a watchful eye, especially when it comes to poaching the perfect egg. If standing in front of a stove with a timer is not your idea of a good time, opt for the Butternut & Swiss Chard Frittata (page 98). A one-pan wonder that can be prepared in advance, or the night before, and assembled in a pinch.

While eggs Benedict are one of the most popular breakfast choices, they are also the most intimidating to make at home. Besides the possibility of your hollandaise splitting, there's also the pound of butter to trip you up. On page 93, I share how to whip up a healthy, less temperamental alternative that is equally lemony and luscious.

For complete feel-good food, head straight for the Avocado Toast (page 90). The Minted Pea & Almond Salsa is bright and crunchy.

For me, there's nothing better than Turkish Eggs (page 94) or the Harissa Chickpea Tartines with Honey Tahini (page 97). Give them a go when you feel like 'travelling'.

GLUTEN-FREE ALMOND BUTTER GRANOLA

Amanda, knowing how you love the Orange & Olive Oil Granola, this recipe is for you. A gluten-free, high-protein breakfast staple. Feel free to customize it by adding free-hand measures of sour cherries and cranberries, or thinly sliced dried pears, for a wintery spin.

MAKES APPROXIMATELY 700 G

150 g coconut flakes
80 g pumpkin seeds
80 g sunflower seeds
45 ml sesame seeds
30 ml flaxseed
30 ml chia seeds
150 g almonds, roughly chopped
2.5 ml ground nutmeg
1.25 ml Maldon sea salt flakes
30 ml olive oil
80 ml honey or maple syrup
45 ml almond butter
5 ml vanilla extract

Preheat the oven to 160°C. Line a large baking sheet with baking paper.

Combine all the dry ingredients in a bowl, up to and including the salt.

Warm the olive oil, honey or maple syrup, almond butter and vanilla in a small pot. Whisk to combine, then add to the dry ingredients. Mix well to coat. Tip onto the baking sheet and spread to ensure even baking.

Bake for 20–22 minutes, turning the granola over several times during the baking time. If you're adding dried fruit, toss through as soon as the granola comes out of the oven.

Cool completely before storing in an airtight container.

ROSEMARY RHUBARB BREAKFAST POTS

Unlike forced rhubarb that grows in the dark, their candy-pink stalks coveted by chefs and bakers the world over, regular rhubarb is less colourful and slightly more tart. Taste and adjust the amount of sugar, depending on the sourness of the fruit and personal preference. I love adding raspberries for complexity and tonal colour.

RHUBARB COMPOTE
MAKES 750 ML

500 g rhubarb, cut into 2 cm batons, rinsed and drained
200 g raspberries
250 ml water
15 ml lemon juice
100 g granulated white sugar
1 vanilla pod, split and scraped
1 sprig of fresh rosemary

BREAKFAST POTS
SERVES 4

375 ml Greek yoghurt
30 ml honey, plus extra to drizzle
2.5 ml vanilla paste or extract
180 ml rhubarb compote
Gluten-free Almond Butter Granola (page 70)
raspberries, to finish

FOR THE COMPOTE, place all the ingredients in a deep saucepan. Bring slowly up to the boil, stirring gently until the sugar is dissolved. Simmer on a medium-low heat for 8–10 minutes. Remove the rosemary sprig and any stray leaves. Transfer to a sterilized jar and set aside to cool. Chill until ready to serve.

FOR THE BREAKFAST POTS, combine the yoghurt, honey and vanilla.

To assemble the pots, portion out 60 ml compote per serving. Top with a handful of granola, then a layer of yoghurt. Finish with raspberries and a drizzle of honey. Serve immediately.

COOK'S NOTE: The recipe for the Rhubarb Compote makes plenty. Store chilled and use for overnight oats or dolloped over vanilla ice cream.

GRAPEFRUIT & GINGER SMOOTHIE

When you have neither time nor inclination for a cooked breakfast, smoothies are the quickest route to racking up your daily quota. To save time, freeze all the ingredients, up to and including the ginger, in a ziplock bag. When you're ready to make your smoothie, cut the frozen fruit into chunks, then add to the blender along with the remaining ingredients. The texture will be creamy and thick, in which case you'll need a spoon.

SERVES 2

2 bananas, peeled, sliced and frozen
1 mango, peeled, cut into cubes and frozen
2 ruby grapefruit, peeled, white pith removed
2 oranges, peeled, white pith removed
zest of 1 orange
15 ml grated fresh ginger
125 ml coconut milk
30 ml honey or maple syrup
2.5 ml vanilla extract
125 ml crushed ice
thinly sliced ruby grapefruit, to finish (optional)

Place all the ingredients, except the ice, in a blender and blitz until smooth.

Add the ice and blend until frothy. Pour into tumblers, add the grapefruit slices if using, and serve immediately.

ANZAC BREAKFAST COOKIES

If you need a portable, on-the-go breakfast, these healthy Anzac cookies are a game-changer. For mornings when your appetite isn't yet fully awake, breakfast cookies are a marvellous thing. Relying on dried fruit and honey for sweetness, they're emphatically oaty and wholesome. If you need a cookie with benefits, this is it.

MAKES 15

- 80 g wholegrain spelt flour
- 60 g cake wheat flour
- 1.25 ml fine salt
- 80 g desiccated coconut
- 140 g porridge oats
- 50 g mixed seeds (pumpkin, flax, sesame and sunflower)
- 70 g dried cranberries
- 4 Medjool dates, pitted and roughly chopped
- 50 g coconut sugar or brown sugar
- 60 ml honey
- 80 ml coconut oil
- 30 ml almond butter
- 2.5 ml bicarbonate of soda combined with 45 ml cold water
- 50 g desiccated coconut, for coating

Preheat the oven to 180°C. Line a large baking sheet with baking paper.

In a mixing bowl, combine the spelt flour, cake wheat flour, salt, coconut, oats, seeds, cranberries and dates.

Place the coconut sugar, honey, oil and nut butter in a small saucepan. Heat until the mixture is bubbling.

Stir in the bicarb water and whisk until frothy. Add the honey mixture to the dry ingredients and mix to combine.

Shape into balls – about 55 g each – and flatten out slightly. Dredge in coconut and arrange on the baking sheet. Bake for 18–20 minutes. Rest for 5 minutes before transferring to a wire rack to cool completely.

COOK'S NOTES: For a vegan option, replace the honey with an equal measure of maple syrup.

Slightly wet hands help when shaping the dough into rounds.

REFINED SUGAR-FREE MUESLI RUSKS

Before I could cook, I was mixing rusks in my mother's enormous, mint-green Tupperware bowl, big as a baby's bathtub. I think they called it The Mix & Store? At the risk of being repetitive, I'm including another rusk recipe in this book and my current favourite – bran-rich, devoid of refined sugars and packed with nuts and seeds. A rather adequate breakfast stand-in.

MAKES ABOUT 40 RUSKS

400 g bran-rich self-raising wheat flour
100 g white self-raising wheat flour
10 ml baking powder
2.5 ml fine salt
5 ml ground cinnamon
120 g porridge oats
90 g desiccated coconut (medium cut)
100 g mixed seeds, plus extra for topping
100 g raw pecans or almonds, roughly chopped
80 g raisins
110 g Medjool dates (7 or 8), pitted and roughly chopped
100 g coconut sugar
60 ml honey
150 g butter or coconut oil, melted
310 ml buttermilk
2 eggs

Preheat the oven to 170°C. Butter and line a 32 x 22 cm baking tin with baking paper.

In a large mixing bowl, combine the bran flour, white self-raising flour, baking powder, salt and cinnamon. Add the oats, coconut, mixed seeds, pecans or almonds, raisins and dates.

To a small saucepan, add the coconut sugar, honey and butter, or coconut oil, if using, and heat, stirring gently until the butter is melted. Remove from the heat, then whisk in the buttermilk. Add the eggs and whisk to combine.

Add the buttermilk mixture to the dry ingredients and mix well. Scrape the dough into the tin and smooth over the top. Scatter with a handful of seeds, pressing them into the dough. Bake for 45 minutes until golden and cooked through.

Cool in the tin for 15 minutes before turning out onto a wire rack. Cover with a tea towel and leave to cool completely. Cut into fingers with a serrated knife and arrange on a lined oven rack. Dry out in a low oven (80°C) for 8 hours. Once cooled, store in an airtight container.

COOK'S NOTE: It's taken me this long to discover that chilling the rusks in the fridge for an hour or two, once cooled, reduces crumbling when sliced.

BROWN BUTTER BUCKWHEAT CRÊPES

Although time consuming, there is nothing difficult about making pancakes. This is how we like them. Supple like dough handkerchiefs, with a deep nuttiness that comes from using browned butter and buckwheat.

MAKES 8–10

40 g butter
75 g buckwheat flour
75 g cake wheat flour
a pinch of fine salt
2 eggs, lightly whisked
250 ml full-cream milk
22.5 ml honey
150 ml water
coconut or vegetable oil, for coating the pan

In a small saucepan, heat the butter over a medium heat. Once the butter is melted, turn the heat up and let it splutter away until nutty and golden in colour. Set aside to cool.

Sift together the buckwheat flour, cake flour and salt. Make a well in the centre, and add the eggs and half the milk. Whisk well to combine, adding the remaining milk in stages to prevent lumps forming. Add the honey, water and cooled butter, and whisk to incorporate.

Cover the batter and rest for at least 30 minutes or overnight.

Heat a non-stick crêpe pan until hot. Coat the pan with a little oil – a paper towel works well.

For a 20 cm pan, pour 60 ml batter into the centre of the pan and swirl quickly to spread. Cook for about 2 minutes, then flip and cook for another minute. Repeat with the remaining batter.

Serve with healthy chocolate Nutella, nut butter or Quick Blueberry Compote (*see* below) and yoghurt.

COOK'S NOTE: The batter keeps well for two days in the fridge. Stir or shake well before using.

QUICK BLUEBERRY COMPOTE In a saucepan, combine 200 g blueberries, 45 ml castor sugar or honey, 15 ml lemon juice and 30 ml water. Bring up to the boil and simmer for 5–7 minutes.

PUMPKIN WAFFLES WITH DATE SYRUP

Pumpkin purée freezes well, which is handy if you like pampoenkoekies or pumpkin pie. Butternut works well too. Roast the unpeeled halves of either in a 180°C oven until tender. Neither oiled, nor salted. Scrape out the softened flesh once cooled. If you don't have a waffle maker, cook as you would pancakes.

MAKES 10

- 75 g white self-raising wheat flour
- 75 g bran-rich self-raising wheat flour
- 5 ml baking powder
- 30 ml castor sugar or honey
- 5 ml ground cinnamon
- a pinch of fine salt
- 2 eggs
- 250 ml buttermilk
- 125 g pumpkin purée
- 30 ml coconut oil or butter, melted
- coconut or vegetable oil, for frying

FOR SERVING

- seasonal fruit (optional)
- Greek yoghurt
- Date Syrup (page 36) or honey

Sift the flours, baking powder, castor sugar, cinnamon and salt into a large mixing bowl.

Place the eggs, buttermilk, pumpkin and coconut oil or butter into a jug and whisk together. Add the wet ingredients to the flour mixture and mix to combine. Cover and chill overnight.

Heat a waffle maker until hot. Brush the surface lightly with coconut or vegetable oil.

Ladle 60 ml batter onto each griddle and cook until golden. Repeat until all the batter is used up.

Serve warm with Quick Caramelized Apples (*see* below), yoghurt and date syrup or honey.

QUICK CARAMELIZED APPLES Heat 15 ml butter or coconut oil and 10 ml honey in a pan. Add thinly sliced apple wedges of 1 apple and caramelize on both sides. Add a cinnamon stick and a splash of water, and reduce until the liquid is syrupy.

BANANA & APPLE MUFFIN LOAF WITH CINNAMON STREUSEL

If you've been staring at those has-beens in the fruit bowl, here's an opportunity for them to shine. Bananas, blackened and miserable, are perfect.

A bakery-style loaf that's borderline cake, but filled with good things.

MAKES 1 LOAF

3 Pink Lady apples
2 very ripe bananas, mashed
60 ml olive oil
60 ml full-cream milk
1 egg
140 g brown sugar
125 g wholegrain spelt flour
60 g buckwheat flour
60 g cake wheat flour
5 ml bicarbonate of soda
2.5 ml baking powder
1.25 ml fine salt
5 ml ground cinnamon
1.25 ml ground cloves

STREUSEL
30 g wholegrain spelt flour
20 g soft brown sugar
30 g whole rolled oats
1.25 ml ground cinnamon
a pinch of fine salt
30 g butter, softened
30 g walnuts, roughly chopped
5 ml cold water

Preheat the oven to 200°C. Line a 25 x 10 cm loaf tin with baking paper.

START BY MAKING THE STREUSEL. In a mixing bowl, combine the spelt flour, sugar, oats, cinnamon and salt. Add the butter and work it through with your fingertips. Mix in the walnuts and water. The mixture should be clumped but not cakey. Set aside.

Peel and cube two of the apples. Leave the skin on the third apple, then halve and thinly slice.

In a large mixing bowl, whisk together the mashed bananas, oil, milk, egg and sugar.

Sift together the spelt flour, buckwheat flour, cake wheat flour, raising agents, salt and spices. Add the banana mixture to the dry ingredients and mix through lightly. Without overmixing, fold in the cubed apples.

Scrape the batter into the tin and smooth over the top. Press the sliced apples into the batter, then scatter over half the streusel. Freeze the rest for later. Bake for 70–75 minutes, or until a skewer inserted comes out clean. Cover loosely with foil for the last 15 minutes of the baking time.

Rest in the tin for 10–15 minutes before turning out onto a wire rack to cool completely.

Serve warm or at room temperature with yoghurt and honey.

MUFFIN OPTION Divide the batter into a 12-hole muffin tin lined with paper cases. Press several apple slices into the batter and top with all the streusel. Bake for 25 minutes before transferring to a wire rack to cool.

FIG TARTINES WITH AMASI LABNEH & ORANGE BLOSSOM TAHINI DRIZZLE

A tartine is essentially an open-faced sandwich. For this sweet version, orange blossom tahini and figs weave their Middle Eastern magic. Delicious too, with macerated strawberries or pears sautéed in maple syrup.

MAKES 2

80 ml Amasi Labneh
2 slices sourdough bread, toasted (rye, wholemeal or seeded)
4–6 figs
a handful of hazelnuts, toasted and roughly chopped
honey, to finish

AMASI LABNEH
1 litre amasi

ORANGE BLOSSOM TAHINI DRIZZLE
15 ml tahini
10 ml honey
2.5 ml orange blossom water
15 ml water

START WITH THE LABNEH by preparing it the night before. Pour the amasi into a muslin-lined sieve set over a bowl. Gather the ends and twist to close, then set aside to drain overnight (if it's very hot, place in the fridge whilst draining). For a thicker consistency, add 4 hours to the draining time. Discard the water and chill the labneh.

FOR THE TAHINI DRIZZLE, place all the ingredients in a small bowl and whisk until smooth.

Spread the labneh onto the warm toast. Slice the figs in half, or quarters if large, and arrange on the labneh. Scatter over the nuts, and drizzle with the tahini sauce and extra honey, if you like. Serve immediately.

COOK'S NOTE: Amasi is a fermented milk, similar to natural yoghurt. You could use thick Greek yoghurt, if making labneh is too much of a schlep.

SUMMER BERRY BRUNCH CRUMBLE

Crumbles are neither tidy nor precise, which makes them all the more appealing. The filling depends on what's in season. Plums and blackberries with a sprig of rosemary are pretty perfect, as are quintessential pie partners, strawberries and rhubarb. Here, the addition of balsamic vinegar lends a deeper tang to the jammy juices. Don't leave it out.

SERVES 6–8

CRUMBLE
50 g wholegrain spelt flour
30 g almond flour
a pinch of fine salt
80 g whole rolled oats
25 g desiccated coconut
30 g almond flakes
45 g castor sugar or coconut sugar
60 g coconut oil or butter, melted
5 ml water

FILLING
550 g mixed summer berries
37.5 ml cornflour
45–60 ml honey, depending on the sweetness of the fruit
45 ml orange juice
15 ml lemon juice
30 ml balsamic vinegar
5 ml vanilla extract

Preheat the oven to 200°C. Butter a 25 cm round baking dish.

FOR THE CRUMBLE topping, combine all the dry ingredients in a mixing bowl. Add the coconut oil or melted butter and the water to the dry ingredients and mix to combine.

FOR THE FILLING, add the mixed berries to a large mixing bowl. Add the cornflour, honey, orange juice, lemon juice, balsamic vinegar and vanilla. Toss lightly to coat. Scrape the fruit, along with any resting juices, into the baking dish. Scatter the crumble on top and bake until golden and crisp, 35–40 minutes.

Cool for 10 minutes before serving. For breakfast and brunch, offer with thick yoghurt and a drizzle of honey. Alternatively, serve with a scoop of vanilla ice cream, if purposed for dessert.

COOK'S NOTE: I use a combination of 200 g strawberries, 250 g blueberries and 100 g raspberries.

AVOCADO TOAST WITH MINTED PEA & ALMOND SALSA

It tastes like spring – fresh and bright. I also use the salsa recipe for a quick summer pasta salad, swapping the almonds for toasted pine nuts. Toss with 400 g cooked pasta and plenty of parmesan. Finish with a drizzle of your best olive oil.

SERVES 4

4 slices of sourdough or ciabatta bread, toasted
20 g rocket
2 ripe avocados, sliced
fine salt and freshly ground black pepper
lemon wedges, to serve (optional)
sprigs of fresh dill, to finish

MINTED PEA & ALMOND SALSA
180 g (roughly 250 ml) garden peas
80 g almonds, roasted and roughly chopped
a large bunch of mint, leaves picked and finely chopped
several sprigs of fresh dill, roughly chopped
zest of 1 lemon
45 ml lemon juice
60 ml extra virgin olive oil
Maldon sea salt flakes and freshly ground black pepper

FIRST MAKE THE SALSA. Place all the ingredients in a small bowl and mix to combine. Season to taste, adjusting with a little more salt or lemon juice.

TO ASSEMBLE, layer the toast with rocket, avocado and the salsa. Add a couple of twists of black pepper and lemon juice, to taste. Finish with sprigs of fresh dill.

HEALTHY EGGS BENEDICT

Replicating butter is impossible, but crafty substitutions produce a fine alternative. Here the hollandaise is light and lemony, a very decent imposter, I think. Turmeric is mainly for colour – the amount is negligible and won't interfere with the taste.

SERVES 2

2 English muffins, toasted
avocado, thinly sliced
fresh rocket
griddled asparagus
prosciutto
baby spinach
poached eggs
a pinch of paprika and chopped fresh chives, to finish

HEALTHY HOLLANDAISE
1 egg yolk
1.25 ml Dijon mustard
15 ml lemon juice
15 ml melted butter
15 ml olive oil
60 ml Greek yoghurt
a knife tip each of cayenne pepper and ground turmeric
fine salt and white pepper, to taste

FIRST MAKE THE HOLLANDAISE. In a heatproof bowl, whisk together the egg yolk, mustard and lemon juice. Set the bowl over a pan of simmering water. Whisk for several minutes until pale and slightly thickened.

Turn off the heat, but leave the pan on the hob. Add the butter and olive oil. Whisk in 15 ml yoghurt to temper the mixture, before adding the remaining yoghurt, cayenne pepper and turmeric. Season to taste with salt and white pepper. For a thinner consistency, add a splash of warm water.

I like to top one muffin half with avocado, rocket and asparagus, and the other with prosciutto, spinach, poached eggs, the whole shebang. Drizzle generously with hollandaise and finish with a pinch of paprika and chopped chives.

COOK'S NOTE: Replace the hollandaise with Goddess Avocado Dressing (page 35).

TURKISH EGGS WITH SPICED BUTTER

Turkish eggs, or *çilbir*, is a dream breakfast – poached eggs served atop lemony yoghurt, swimming in spicy oils. Finish with za'atar, a Middle Eastern thyme and sesame seed spice blend, which adds lively contrast and a little crunch. Warm bread is a requisite.

SERVES 2

SPICED BUTTER
30 ml butter
30 ml olive oil
2.5 ml each of ground cumin, ground coriander, paprika and dried red chilli flakes
a pinch of Maldon sea salt flakes and freshly ground black pepper

TO SERVE
pita bread
olive oil, for brushing
15 ml za'atar, plus extra to finish
250 ml Greek yoghurt
zest of ½ lemon
soft poached eggs
fresh dill sprigs, to finish

START WITH THE SPICED BUTTER. In a small saucepan, heat the butter, oil and spices until bubbling. Season with salt and black pepper. Set aside and keep warm.

Brush the pita bread lightly on both sides with olive oil. Scatter over the za'atar. Toast in a hot pan until golden.

Combine the yoghurt and lemon zest, and divide between two warmed plates. Top with the eggs, then drizzle over the warm spiced butter. Finish with za'atar and dill.

Serve immediately with the warm pitas.

HARISSA CHICKPEA TARTINES WITH HONEY TAHINI SAUCE

If you have the first cookbook, you'll know I'm severely gripped by harissa and tahini. We're using both. And sourdough bread. Does it get any better? Double-batch the chickpeas and keep half for a grim weathered morning when a spicy, warm breakfast is just what you need.

MAKES 8

HARISSA CHICKPEAS
1 large red onion, finely diced
olive oil, for cooking
1 clove garlic, minced
30 ml harissa paste
15 ml tomato paste
1 x 400 g tin chopped tomatoes
125 ml vegetable stock
10 ml lemon juice
100 g baby spinach
1 x 400 g tin chickpeas, rinsed and drained
fine salt and freshly ground black pepper, to taste

HONEY TAHINI SAUCE
60 ml each of tahini, cold water and Greek yoghurt
30 ml lemon juice
5 ml honey
fine salt, to taste

TARTINES
8 slices of rye sourdough, toasted and brushed with olive oil
50 g grated sharp cheddar or crumbled feta
black and white sesame seeds, to finish

FOR THE HARISSA CHICKPEAS, sauté the onion in 15 ml olive oil until softened, about 10 minutes. Stir in the garlic and cook for another minute. Add the harissa, tomato paste and chopped tomatoes. Pour in the stock and lemon juice. Cover and simmer for 20–25 minutes.

Add the spinach and wilt down before adding the chickpeas. Season with salt and black pepper. Cook for another 5 minutes.

IN THE MEANTIME, whisk together the ingredients for the honey tahini sauce in a small bowl.

TO ASSEMBLE, spoon the chickpeas over the toasted sourdough. Drizzle 10 ml honey tahini sauce over each. Scatter with cheese and sesame seeds. Grill until golden and bubbling, 5–6 minutes. Serve with the remaining honey tahini sauce alongside.

BUTTERNUT & SWISS CHARD FRITTATA

Donna Hay once said that if you have eggs in your fridge, you have a meal. And she's right.

With the dexterity to straddle breakfast, lunch and supper, frittatas facilitate a good fridge clear-out – less-than-perfect vegetables and chunks of cheese left over from Saturday night's drinks are all fair game. The addition of dairy (yoghurt, cream or milk) ensures the egg is fluffy and light.

SERVES 6

1 medium butternut, peeled and roughly chopped
olive oil, for roasting and cooking
2.5 ml ground mixed spice
fine salt and freshly ground black pepper
1 shallot, finely diced
3 leeks, sliced into penny rounds
200 g Swiss chard or spinach, roughly chopped
a pinch of ground nutmeg
zest of ½ lemon

BASIC EGG CUSTARD
7 eggs
125 ml Greek yoghurt
5 ml wholegrain mustard
5 ml dried oregano
fine salt and freshly ground black pepper
50 g mature cheddar cheese, grated
butter, for greasing

TOPPING
100 g goat's milk cheese
15 ml pine nuts

Preheat the oven to 220°C.

Arrange the butternut in a roasting tin and drizzle with 30 ml olive oil. Season with mixed spice, salt and black pepper. Toss to coat, then roast for 40 minutes.

Heat 15 ml oil in a pan and sauté the shallot until softened. Add the leeks and cook for several minutes more. Working in batches, add half the Swiss Chard or spinach, allowing it to wilt down before adding the next handful. Add the nutmeg and lemon zest. Season lightly with salt and black pepper.

FOR THE EGG CUSTARD, whisk together the eggs, yoghurt, mustard and oregano. Season with salt and black pepper. Stir in the grated cheddar.

Butter a 25 cm round ovenproof dish. Place the wilted spinach mixture on the base and top with roasted butternut. Pour over the egg custard. Dot with goat's milk cheese and pine nuts. Bake until the top is golden and puffed, around 35 minutes.

ZA'ATAR SPANAKOPITA

When my daughter, Skylar, said Fournos Bakery makes *the* best spanakopita, I went out and bought three boxes of phyllo pastry and a boot-load of fresh spinach. She ate five of the eight slices. I feel much better now.

Possibly the most delicious thing you can do with spinach. Adding leeks, baby marrows and za'atar expands the flavours from within, and on top.

SERVES 10

olive oil, for cooking
2 medium leeks, rinsed and sliced
5 medium baby marrows, coarsely grated
400 g young spinach, rinsed, drained and roughly chopped
a pinch of ground nutmeg
fine salt and freshly ground black pepper
3 spring onions, sliced
zest of 1 lemon
a generous handful each of mint and flat-leaf parsley, roughly chopped
250 g feta, crumbled
100 g ricotta, crumbled
22.5 ml za'atar
2 eggs, lightly whisked
250 g phyllo pastry
100 g butter, melted, plus extra for greasing
15 ml sesame seeds combined with 15 ml za'atar, to finish

Heat 15 ml olive oil in a wide-based pan. Sauté the leeks until softened, 8–10 minutes. Add the baby marrows and cook for several more minutes. Add the spinach in batches, allowing it to wilt down before adding the next handful. Season with nutmeg, salt and black pepper. Remove from the heat and stir in the spring onions, lemon zest, mint and parsley. Set aside to cool.

In a mixing bowl, combine the feta, ricotta, 22.5 ml za'atar and the eggs. Stir in the spinach mixture lightly.

Preheat the oven to 200°C. Brush the base and sides of a 32 x 22 cm baking tin with butter.

Cut each phyllo sheet in half, or to fit. Brush each sheet lightly with butter before layering into the tin. For the base, use seven sheets.

Spread all the filling evenly over the base. Top with eight sheets of phyllo, brushing each sheet with butter before layering.

Score the pastry into the size or shape desired. Brush the top layer with butter, then scatter over the sesame seed and za'atar mix.

For the scrunched collar, cut two phyllo sheets into six equal strips. Brush with butter and scrunch together to form a collar.

Bake for 35–40 minutes. Cover loosely with foil for the last 5–8 minutes, if the top is browning too much. Cool for at least 10 minutes before serving.

WELL-ROOTED

–PLANT-RICH SALADS & SIDES–

Salads – where colour and texture exist in glorious abundance. Led by the rhythms of seasonality, there is no better playground for wholesome and delicious. This is when food is at its happiest and most beautiful.

If you don't like nuts, kale, chickpeas or tahini, buckle up! By the end of the chapter, I hope you'll be smitten with their vibrant personalities and unique flavours they bring to plant-centred eating. Maybe it's time to explore the unfamiliar, starting with the Ruby Jewel Spoon Salad (page 106). It's sensational. Next time, I'll throw in some goat's milk cheese or feta, for salty contrast. Many of the salads include a combination of raw, cooked or roasted vegetables – the play between each is hugely appealing.

Some of the best salads begin with what you already have in the fridge. Besides leafy greens, think of herbs as flavour provocateurs, rather than a garnishing afterthought. To revive tired herbs, soak them in a bowl of ice water for 10 minutes, then shake off the excess water and you're good to go.

Dressings, sauces and pestos are a great way to use up excess herbs – see the Pantry & Larder chapter on page 8. When it comes to dressing salads, especially leafy ones, leave this to just before serving. Grain salads, though, need a little more time to absorb the surrounding flavours – 20–30 minutes in advance should be ample time.

A WORD ON GRAIN BOWLS

- Ensure grains – rice, barley, quinoa, bulgur wheat – are 'air-dried' before combining with other ingredients.
- Always toast nuts and seeds to ramp up their flavour. Add these crunchy bits just before serving.
- Citrus zest – lemons, limes and oranges add heaps of zing to dressings. Include both the zest and the juice when making a dressing.
- A smidge of honey does wonders to soften the acidity of lemon and vinegar. Maple syrup, date syrup or pomegranate molasses are great substitutes, too.

RUBY JEWEL SPOON SALAD

The combination is sort of quirky, but in a brilliantly simple way. Eating salad with a spoon is rather appealing. It suggests an ease that does away with forking uncooperative fiddly bits, while at the same time ensuring a complete mouthful of all the components.

SERVES 6

250 g cherry tomatoes, halved
200 g strawberries, hulled and quartered
1 red sweet pepper, deseeded and finely diced
1 shallot or ½ small red onion, finely diced
85 g pomegranate seeds
25 g dried cranberries
1 red chilli, seeds in or scraped (depending on heat preferred), and finely diced

DRESSING
5 ml coriander seeds, toasted and finely ground
5 ml sumac
15 ml lemon juice
30 ml extra virgin olive oil
15 ml pomegranate molasses or honey
fine salt and freshly ground black pepper
25 g fresh herbs (mint and flat-leaf parsley), roughly chopped

Combine the tomatoes, strawberries, red pepper, shallot or red onion, pomegranate seeds, cranberries and chilli in a mixing bowl.

FOR THE DRESSING, whisk together the coriander, sumac, lemon juice, olive oil and pomegranate molasses or honey. Season lightly with salt and black pepper.

Add the herbs to the salad and pour over the dressing. Toss lightly to combine.

COOK'S NOTE: Replace the sumac with the zest of 1 lemon. Serve with lamb, hummus and flatbreads, or grilled fish and chicken.

QUINOA DETOX CRUNCH BOWL

This is how I love to eat – vibrantly fresh and colourful. While vegetable yields are never exact, dressing amounts are specific, so taste and adjust until there's a harmonious balance of salt, acid and oil. Add the Miso Tahini Drizzle (page 126) if the idea of a creamy element appeals.

SERVES 6

- 150 g mixed quinoa, cooked as per manufacturer's instructions, and cooled
- 2 large carrots, scrubbed and grated
- 1 each of red and yellow sweet peppers, deseeded and diced
- 100 g mixed leaves (spinach, rocket and watercress), roughly chopped
- a generous handful of fresh flat-leaf parsley and mint, leaves picked and roughly chopped
- 1 x 400 g tin chickpeas, rinsed and drained
- 75 g dried cranberries
- 100 g feta, crumbled
- 1 x quantity Orange & Coriander Vinaigrette (page 28)
- 50 g almonds, toasted and roughly chopped

Place the cooled quinoa in a large mixing bowl. Add all the remaining salad ingredients, except the vinaigrette and almonds.

Make the vinaigrette, drizzle it over the salad and toss to coat. Add the almonds just before serving.

CITRUS SALAD WITH BURRATA & DUKKAH

Barely a recipe and more of an assembly than actual work. Citrus is a feisty opponent and challenges the richness of the cream-stuffed mozzarella. It's bold yet simple. Prepare the citrus and vinaigrette ahead of time, and the fennel just before serving. If you don't have dukkah, replace it with toasted pistachio nuts – they're equally scrumptious.

SERVES 4 AS A STARTER

1 orange, peeled and sliced
1 ruby grapefruit, peeled and sliced
1 pomelo, peeled and segmented
1 x quantity Orange & Coriander Vinaigrette (page 28)
2 fennel bulbs, woody core removed, and thinly sliced
2 burrata balls
dukkah, to finish
pomegranate seeds, to finish
fennel sprigs, to finish

Arrange the citrus on a serving plate. Make the vinaigrette and drizzle a little over the fennel, then add to the citrus segments.

Place the burrata on top. Drizzle with more vinaigrette. Finish with dukkah, pomegranate seeds and fennel sprigs.

COOK'S NOTE: You need only half the vinaigrette here. Use the remainder for a quick clear-out-the-fridge salad.

KITCHEN STAPLE BALSAMIC ROAST TOMATOES

I've made these tomatoes a thousand times. I suppose that's what makes it a staple. Spoon hot tomatoes over cold yoghurt, Ottolenghi-style, or pile on bruschetta or alongside scrambled eggs. They're great for a quick Tomato Soup, too (*see* below). If you plan on making the soup, add 2 or 3 cloves of garlic to the roasting tin.

SERVES 4–6

500 g cherry tomatoes, halved
several sprigs of fresh thyme
30 ml olive oil, for roasting
5 ml herbes de Provence
2.5 ml dried red chilli flakes
fine salt and freshly ground black pepper
15 ml balsamic vinegar

Preheat the oven to 200°C.

Arrange the tomatoes and thyme in a roasting tin. Drizzle over the olive oil.

Scatter over the herbs and chilli flakes. Season with salt and black pepper, and toss to coat.

Roast for 40–45 minutes. Drizzle over the balsamic vinegar and swirl the tray gently to coat.

QUICK TOMATO SOUP Make a double quantity of Kitchen Staple Balsamic Roast Tomatoes. Remove the thyme sprigs and scrape the roasted tomatoes into a blender. Add 600–650 ml warm stock and blitz until smooth. Pour into a saucepan, add 60 ml fresh cream or mascarpone and heat through. Season with salt and black pepper to taste.

PAPRIKA & HONEY ROAST PUMPKIN

Most of us have a handful of reliable sides on regular rotation. They're consistently good and, mostly, simple. This is ours. Nothing fancy, but far from ordinary. I leave the skin on, as it holds the flesh together. Roasting at a high temperature encourages deep caramelization, like pumpkin toffee-apples.

SERVES 6

1 medium butternut, cut into rounds, then halved
1 pumpkin, cut into wedges
2 red onions, cut into wedges
3 sprigs of fresh rosemary
fresh sage leaves (be generous here, at least 20)
45 ml olive oil, plus extra to finish
30 ml honey
10 ml smoked paprika
2.5 ml dried red chilli flakes
fine salt and freshly ground black pepper

Preheat the oven to 220°C.

Arrange the butternut, pumpkin and onions on a large roasting tin. Add the rosemary and sage, tucking some underneath the vegetables, then drizzle with 45 ml olive oil and the honey. Season with paprika, chilli, salt and black pepper.

Roast for 45–50 minutes, turning over the vegetables 10 minutes before the end of the cooking time. Drizzle with a little extra olive oil just before serving.

COOK'S NOTE: The skin of Japanese Hokkaido pumpkin (also known as red kuri squash) is soft and edible once roasted, and the flesh sweet and creamy. (Available at Woolworths.)

QUICK BUTTER BEAN MASH WITH DILL SALSA

With a similar texture to hummus, this mash/dip is good with pita breads or sliced beef fillet. The dill salsa with briny capers and fresh herbs livens things up immensely.

SERVES 6 AS A DIP

2 x 400 g tins butter beans, rinsed and drained
30 ml extra virgin olive oil
30 ml lemon juice
fine salt and freshly ground black pepper

DILL SALSA
a generous handful each of fresh basil, dill and flat-leaf parsley, leaves picked
30 ml capers, rinsed and drained
60 ml extra virgin olive oil
30 ml lemon juice
fine salt and freshly ground black pepper

For the mash, place the butter beans, olive oil and lemon juice in a processor. Blitz until smooth and creamy. Season with salt and pepper, and pulse to combine.

TO MAKE THE DILL SALSA, bundle the herbs together and chop roughly. In a small bowl, combine the herbs, capers, olive oil and lemon juice. Season with salt and black pepper.

Swirl the butter bean spread onto a plate and drizzle over the salsa.

EVERYDAY NUTTY BULGUR WHEAT SALAD

A hard-working staple that will serve you well. You really want the nuts to be crunchy, so add these just before you're ready to serve. Pair this salad with the Chicken Tagine with Almond & Preserved Lemon Salsa (page 220) or Saffron & Honey Roast Lamb with Preserved Lemon & Dates (page 167).

SERVES 6

1 x quantity Classic Vinaigrette (page 28)
150 g bulgur wheat
3.75 ml ground cumin
2.5 ml stock powder (vegetable or chicken stock)
fine salt and freshly ground black pepper, to taste
40 g fresh rocket
a very generous handful each of fresh flat-leaf parsley and mint
3–4 spring onions, thinly sliced
50 g walnuts, toasted and roughly chopped
45 g sunflower seeds, toasted
fresh rocket and mint, to finish

Start by making the vinaigrette.

Place the bulgur wheat, cumin, stock powder and a pinch of salt in a heatproof mixing bowl. Add just enough boiling water to cover the wheat. Stir through quickly, then cover with cling film. Set aside for 10 minutes. Once cooled, fluff the grains with a fork.

Bundle half the rocket and all the herbs together on a board, and chop roughly. Scrape into the wheat, along with the spring onions and remaining rocket. Add the walnuts and sunflower seeds.

Drizzle over the vinaigrette and toss lightly to coat. Adjust the seasoning to taste, and finish with fresh rocket and mint.

AVOCADO & EDAMAME GARDEN SALAD

The secret to a really good green salad is the freshest produce and a vigorous dressing to make it shine. After slicing the baby marrows, a gentle pat down with paper towel will ensure the dressing clings. Toss at the table, or there-about. Next time, I'll add fried halloumi strips for a salty contrast.

SERVES 2 AS A LIGHT LUNCH
OR 4 AS A SIDE

½ x quantity Classic Vinaigrette (page 28)
100 g shelled edamame beans
3 small baby marrows, sliced into ribbons
1 Mediterranean cucumber, thinly sliced
a generous handful each of baby spinach and rocket
30 g toasted sunflower and pumpkin seeds mix
fine salt and freshly ground black pepper
1 avocado, halved, pitted and sliced
micro herbs and pea shoots, to finish

Start by making the vinaigrette.

Combine the edamame, baby marrows, cucumber, spinach, rocket and seeds in a bowl. Season lightly with salt and black pepper. Drizzle over half the dressing and toss to coat.

Divide between two plates. Add the avocado, micro herbs and pea shoots. Drizzle over the remaining dressing and serve immediately.

GREEN FATTOUSH WITH ZA'ATAR & MINT VINAIGRETTE

A modern take on fattoush with heaps of glorious greens. It exists happily as a stand-alone vegetarian main, perhaps with hummus and warm pita breads. Alternatively, offer with Harissa & Sumac Chicken Kebabs (page 162).

SERVES 6–8

100 g bulgur wheat
2.5 ml vegetable stock powder
90 g white quinoa, cooked as per manufacturer's instructions
1 Mediterranean cucumber or half an English cucumber, deseeded and diced
3 medium baby marrows, coarsely grated, excess water squeezed out
100 g young spinach
40 g fresh rocket
a generous handful of fresh mint, flat-leaf parsley and dill
3 spring onions, thinly sliced
100 g feta, crumbled
50 g dried cranberries
40 g currants
2 pita breads, toasted and broken into shards (*see* below)
120 g seeds and nuts, toasted (I like sunflower, pumpkin and almond flakes)
1 x quantity Za'atar & Mint Vinaigrette (page 28)
micro herbs, to finish (optional)

Place the bulgur wheat in a heatproof bowl. Add the stock powder and season lightly with salt. Pour over just enough boiling water to cover the wheat. Cover tightly and set aside to rehydrate for 10 minutes, then fluff with a fork.

Place the cooked quinoa and bulgur wheat in a large mixing bowl. Add the cucumber and baby marrows, and toss to break up the grated marrows.

Pile the spinach, rocket and herbs together on a chopping board. Chop roughly, then add to the grains along with the spring onions, feta, cranberries and currants. Add the pita chips, and two-thirds of the seeds and almond flakes.

Whisk together the ingredients for the vinaigrette, then drizzle over the salad, tossing lightly to coat.

Transfer the salad to a serving plate. Scatter over the remaining seeds and almonds.

PITA SHARDS Slice each pita in half horizontally. Brush both sides with olive oil and season with salt, pepper and dried oregano. Bake for 10 minutes at 180°C, turn them over and bake for a further 5 minutes.

KALE & AVOCADO SALAD WITH TAHINI CAESAR DRESSING

The chickpeas don't necessarily need to be crisp. It's more about getting the spices to stick. If you're struggling with kale, this is the recipe to help hurdle the fence. My husband thought kale was for girls, until he tasted this. You'll possibly have pangrattato left over, in which case, try to squeeze the Chicken & Chorizo Rigatoni (page 149) into your meal plan the following week.

SERVES 6

SIMPLE PANGRATTATO
30 ml olive oil
200 g day-old breadcrumbs (sourdough or ciabatta)
zest of 1 lemon
several sprigs of fresh thyme, leaves picked
1 sprig of fresh rosemary, leaves picked and finely chopped
Maldon sea salt flakes and freshly ground black pepper

SALAD
olive oil, for cooking
1 x 400 g tin chickpeas, rinsed and drained
2.5 ml paprika
5 ml ground cumin
fine salt and freshly ground black pepper
½ bunch curly kale, centre rib removed, and roughly torn
extra virgin olive oil, to drizzle
30 ml lemon juice
40 g fresh rocket
20 g micro herbs
50 g walnuts, toasted and roughly chopped
45 g pumpkin seeds, toasted
50 g parmesan shavings
1–2 avocados, cut into large cubes
1 x quantity Tahini Caesar Dressing (page 27)

FOR THE PANGRATTATO, heat the oil in a wide-based pan. Add the breadcrumbs and toast over a medium heat until golden, 12–15 minutes. Add the remaining ingredients and toast for another minute or two. Set aside to cool and crisp up.

FOR THE SALAD, drizzle 15 ml olive oil over the chickpeas. Season with paprika, cumin, salt and black pepper. Pan-fry over a medium-high heat for 5–6 minutes. Set aside to cool.

Place the kale in a large mixing bowl. Drizzle over 15 ml olive oil and 15 ml lemon juice. Massage the kale gently to soften.

Add the chickpeas, rocket, micro herbs, walnuts, pumpkin seeds and half the parmesan. Drizzle with a little more olive oil and the remaining lemon juice. Season lightly with salt and black pepper. Add the avocado and toss through gently. Transfer to a serving plate. Top with the remaining parmesan and the pangrattato crumbs.

Drizzle over half the Tahini Caesar Dressing, serving the remainder alongside.

ROAST BUTTERNUT WITH MISO TAHINI DRIZZLE & TOASTY SEED SPRINKLES

One of those dishes that are best served warm or at room temperature. Never fridge cold. It takes restraint not to drizzle the sauce over everything. It's addictively smooth and creamy.

SERVES 4 AS A SIDE

500 g butternut, peeled and roughly chopped
olive oil, for roasting
3.75 ml ground mixed spice
fine salt and freshly ground black pepper
Toasty Seed Sprinkles, to finish (page 25)
sumac, to finish

MISO TAHINI DRIZZLE
60 ml tahini
10 ml miso paste
60 ml Greek yoghurt
30 ml lemon juice
60–80 ml water, depending on preferred consistency

Preheat the oven to 220°C. Line and grease a large roasting tin.

Arrange the butternut in the roasting tin. Drizzle with olive oil and season with mixed spice, salt and black pepper. Roast for 40–45 minutes until caramelized.

FOR THE DRIZZLE, place all the ingredients in a bowl and whisk together until smooth. Season lightly with salt and plenty of black pepper.

To serve, swirl half the drizzle onto a serving plate. Top with the butternut. Spoon over a little more of the drizzle, then finish with Toasty Seed Sprinkles and a pinch of sumac.

ROAST SWEET POTATOES WITH BROWN BUTTER MISO & SUNFLOWER SEED CLUSTERS

Meaty, in a vegetal sort of way. Admittedly, there are several steps, none of which are complicated. The miso butter is borderline Marmite, with a heat that's there, but hardly fierce. Rich and intensely flavourful.

SERVES 4–6

4–5 large sweet potatoes, scrubbed and sliced into rounds
olive oil, for roasting
2.5 ml ground mixed spice
5 ml cumin seeds
5 ml smoked paprika
fine salt and freshly ground black pepper

BROWN BUTTER MISO
40 g butter
2 sprigs of fresh rosemary, leaves picked
2.5 ml dried red chilli flakes
10 ml honey
7.5 ml lemon juice
10 ml miso paste
10 ml water
Maldon sea salt flakes and freshly ground black pepper

SUNFLOWER SEED CLUSTERS
40 g sunflower seeds
15 ml each of black and white sesame seeds
15 ml honey
Maldon sea salt flakes and freshly ground black pepper

GOAT'S MILK CHEESE YOGHURT
100 g goat's milk cheese
250 ml Greek yoghurt
zest of 1 small lemon

Preheat the oven to 200°C. Line a roasting tin with baking paper. Arrange the sweet potatoes in the tin. Drizzle with olive oil and season with mixed spice, cumin, paprika, salt and black pepper. Roast for 45–50 minutes, turning over the potatoes after 35 minutes.

FOR THE MISO BUTTER, melt the butter, along with the rosemary and chilli, in a small saucepan. Swirl from time to time until the rosemary is crisp and the butter browned. Remove from the heat. Add the remaining ingredients and whisk with a balloon whisk to combine. Set aside, reheating just before serving.

FOR THE SEED CLUSTERS, toast the sunflower seeds in a dry pan. Once golden, add the sesame seeds and toast for another minute or two. Drizzle over the honey and toss to coat. Cook until the honey caramelizes. Season with sea salt flakes and black pepper. Scrape onto a plate to cool.

TO MAKE THE GOAT'S MILK CHEESE YOGHURT, place all the ingredients in a processor and blitz briefly to combine.

Spread the yoghurt onto a serving plate. Arrange the warm sweet potatoes on top. Drizzle over the miso butter and top with the sunflower seed clusters.

ROAST CAULIFLOWER STEAKS WITH CASHEW SAUCE & PANGRATTATO

The sauce is insane, as too are the crunchy crumbs. If you have vegetarian or vegan friends, or want to wow your guests, this is one to make. Use any leftover sauce to drizzle over roast broccoli or cabbage wedges.

SERVES 4

- 1 head cauliflower, sliced into 2.5 cm steaks
- olive oil, for roasting
- fine salt and freshly ground black pepper
- 15 ml lemon juice
- Simple Pangrattato (page 124), to finish
- extra virgin olive oil, to drizzle
- a handful of fresh mint, roughly chopped

CASHEW SAUCE
MAKES 250 ML

- 180 ml boiling water
- 100 g cashew nuts, toasted
- 30 ml nutritional yeast
- 1 clove garlic, roasted
- 2.5 ml smoked paprika
- 60 ml olive oil
- 15 ml lemon juice
- 2.5–3.75 ml Maldon sea salt flakes
- plenty of freshly ground black pepper

Preheat the oven to 200°C.

Brush both sides of the cauliflower steaks with olive oil. Season with salt and black pepper.

Heat a large non-stick ovenproof pan until hot. Cook the cauliflower, without lifting, until golden, about 5 minutes. Turn and brown on the other side. Drizzle over the lemon juice, then roast in the preheated oven for about 20 minutes.

IN THE MEANTIME, PREPARE THE SAUCE. Pour the boiling water over the cashews and set aside for 20 minutes to soften.

Transfer the cashews and soaking water to a blender. Add the remaining ingredients, and blitz until smooth and silky. Be generous with the pepper.

TO SERVE, swirl a quarter of the sauce onto a large plate. Arrange the cauliflower on top, then drizzle with a little more sauce. Scatter over as much pangrattato as you like. A lot is good! Finish with a light drizzle of olive oil and the chopped mint.

QUICK & SLOW

–MIDDAY & DINNER PLATES–

It's here, halfway between Monday and the weekend, when most of us fall into the rut of habitual comfort. Let's get unstuck and expand our go-to recipe repertoire. In this chapter we balance the busyness of weekdays with slower weekends, when gentler hours in the kitchen are just what we need.

Weeknight suppers are not about perfection. We're aiming for deliciousness. Nothing too fussy or complicated. Home cooking needs to ooze comfort and approachability.

There are some recipes – Goan Mince & Potato Pastries (page 163) – that are a little more trouble, but abundantly worth it. As is the Saffron & Honey Roast Lamb with Preserved Lemon & Dates (page 167), which will have you hatching plans of who next to invite to dinner so that you can make it again.

In some instances, the ingredient lists may look extensive, but the method, a quick throw together. We rely heavily on dried spices and the pantry to build layers of flavour. With a crafty concoction of spices, you can make just about anything taste good.

Assuming parmesan is a permanent fixture in your fridge – or similar sharply spiked cheese – head straight for the pastas. There are several to choose from – a blender pesto, an oven-roasted sauce and a Chicken & Chorizo Rigatoni (page 149), a recipe I return to time and again. Double-batching pasta sauces – and soups – should be a given. Cook once, eat twice.

ROAST ALMOND GAZPACHO WITH PICKLED GRAPES

A rich and creamy soup that requires small portions. Chilling overnight allows the flavours to mellow, so make it the day before you plan on serving. Use blanched almonds for a smoother finish. Roasting the garlic softens its sharpness, which I think is rather lovely in this instance.

SERVES 6–8 (YIELDS 800 ML)

ALMOND GAZPACHO
150 g blanched almonds
100 g fresh white breadcrumbs
1 clove garlic, roasted
500 ml cold water
125 ml coconut milk
30 ml extra virgin olive oil, plus extra to finish
15 ml white prosecco vinegar or apple cider vinegar
10 ml lemon juice
3.75 ml Maldon sea salt flakes
white pepper, to taste

PICKLING LIQUID
125 ml water
125 ml apple cider vinegar
5 ml fine salt
5 ml castor sugar
2.5 ml coriander seeds
5 ml pink peppercorns
3.75 ml fennel seeds

100 g (1 small bunch) seedless grapes, thinly sliced
30 ml almond flakes, toasted, to finish

FOR THE GAZPACHO, preheat the oven to 180°C. Arrange the almonds on a small baking sheet and roast until golden, 8–10 minutes. Toss the almonds once or twice whilst roasting. Set aside to cool.

Tip the almonds into a blender. Add the breadcrumbs, garlic, water and coconut milk. Blitz until smooth. Season to taste with salt and white pepper, then stir in the olive oil, vinegar and lemon juice. Strain, then cover and chill overnight.

FOR THE PICKLING LIQUID, place all the ingredients in a small saucepan. Heat gently until the salt and sugar dissolve. Remove from the heat and add the grapes. Pour into a small bowl and set aside to cool.

To serve, ladle small portions of gazpacho into serving glasses or bowls. With a slotted spoon, remove the grapes from the liquid, draining excess liquid on paper towels.

Spoon the pickled grapes over the soup and scatter with almond flakes. Drizzle over a little extra virgin olive oil to finish.

HEALING CABBAGE SOUP

A friend recently shared her cabbage soup recipe with me. It's clean eating, the kind that restores balance, especially helpful when you've fallen off the weekend wagon or simply want more veggies in your life. The fact that it's freezer-friendly adds to its morality.

SERVES 8–10

- extra virgin olive oil, for cooking and drizzling
- 1 brown onion, diced
- 2 cloves garlic, minced
- 2 sprigs of fresh rosemary, leaves picked and roughly chopped
- zest of 1 lemon
- 3 carrots, peeled and roughly chopped
- 3 stalks celery with leaves on, sliced
- 1 fennel bulb, hard core removed, and sliced
- 1 red sweet pepper, deseeded and roughly chopped
- 3 medium baby marrows, sliced
- 1 small green cabbage, shredded (about 625 ml)
- fine salt and freshly ground black pepper
- 5 ml dried oregano
- 2.5 ml dried red chilli flakes
- 1.5 litre vegetable or chicken stock
- 1 parmesan rind (optional)
- za'atar, to finish
- Toasty Seed Sprinkles (page 25), to finish

Heat 30 ml olive oil in a large saucepan. Sauté the onion until soft and translucent, about 10 minutes. Stir in the garlic, rosemary and lemon zest, and cook for another 2 minutes.

Add the carrots, celery, fennel, red pepper, baby marrows and cabbage. Season lightly with salt and black pepper. Cook over a medium heat until the vegetables have softened slightly, around 10 minutes should do. Add the oregano, chilli, stock and parmesan rind. Bring the soup up to the boil, cover with a lid and simmer until the vegetables are completely tender. Set aside to cool slightly.

Remove the parmesan rind and discard. Transfer the soup to a blender and pureé in batches until smooth.

Return the soup to the pan and heat through. Taste and adjust seasoning, if needed.

Serve with a drizzle of extra virgin olive oil, za'atar and seed sprinkles for an extra hit of flavour.

COOK'S NOTE: Omit the parmesan rind if you're wanting to make it vegan and replace with a heaped tablespoon of nutritional yeast flakes at the end of the cooking time.

BUTTERNUT & LEEK SOUP WITH BROWNED CHILLI BUTTER

You'll notice browned butter popping up throughout the book. And yes, it is worth the hype. Once browned, the flavour becomes intensely nutty.

Comforting fire-front food.

MAKES 2.4 LITRES (BATCH COOKING)

1 kg butternut chunks
300 g orange sweet potato, peeled and roughly chopped
2 large carrots, peeled and roughly chopped
olive oil, for roasting and cooking
7.5 ml ground coriander
fine salt and freshly ground black pepper
3 medium leeks, well rinsed and cut into rounds
2 long stalks celery, thinly sliced
15 ml freshly grated ginger
zest of 1 orange
125 ml orange juice
1.25 litres vegetable stock
1 x 400 g tin coconut milk
15 ml lemon juice
60 ml fresh cream, to serve
roasted hazelnuts, roughly chopped, to finish (optional)

BROWNED CHILLI BUTTER
50 g butter
30 ml lemon juice
a pinch of saffron threads
zest of 1 lemon
10 ml honey
2.5 ml dried red chilli flakes
Maldon sea salt flakes, to season

TO MAKE THE SOUP, preheat the oven to 200°C. Arrange the butternut, sweet potatoes and carrots in a large roasting tin. Drizzle with olive oil and season with coriander, salt and black pepper. Roast for 50 minutes.

Heat 30 ml olive oil in a large saucepan. Add the leeks and celery and sauté over a low heat until softened, 10–12 minutes. Stir in the ginger, orange zest and orange juice. Add the roast vegetables along with the stock and coconut milk. Bring up to the boil, cover with the lid, then simmer for around 25 minutes.

Purée the soup with an immersion blender until smooth. Add 180–250 ml hot water to thin out the consistency. Taste and adjust seasoning if needed, then stir in the lemon juice.

TO MAKE THE BROWNED BUTTER, heat the butter in a small saucepan over a medium-high heat. Once the butter is melted, turn the heat up and let it splutter away until nutty and golden in colour. Set aside to cool.

Heat the lemon juice until warm. Add the saffron, lemon zest, honey and chilli flakes. Set aside to infuse for 10 minutes. Stir in the browned butter and season lightly with salt.

To serve, ladle the soup into warm bowls. Drizzle with cream and browned chilli butter, and scatter over the hazelnuts, if using.

HARIRA VEGETABLE SOUP WITH SORGHUM & QUINOA

Traditionally made with lamb and eaten during Ramadan to break the fast. I've given this hearty soup a vegan makeover. My eldest daughter Skylar, who by her own admission is the fussiest of eaters, declared it the best soup ever. With this winning ticket in hand, I've made it again and again. The minted walnut salsa is optional but really good. Lovely stuff!

MAKES 2.4 LITRES

70 g sorghum
olive oil, for cooking
1 large brown onion, finely diced
2 stalks celery, finely sliced
3 carrots, peeled and finely sliced
2 cloves garlic, minced
15 ml freshly grated ginger
zest of 1 lemon
5 ml paprika
10 ml ground cumin
5 ml ground coriander
5 ml ground turmeric
45 ml tomato paste
2 x 400 g tins chopped tomatoes
120 g red lentils, rinsed and drained
1.6 litres vegetable stock
50 g quinoa, rinsed and drained
1 x 400 g tin chickpeas, rinsed and drained
15 ml lemon juice

MINTED WALNUT SALSA

a generous handful each of fresh flat-leaf parsley and mint, roughly chopped
30 g walnuts, toasted and roughly chopped
zest of 1 lemon
juice of ½ lemon
5 ml honey
60 ml extra virgin olive oil
fine salt and freshly ground black pepper

Start the night before by soaking the sorghum in water. Rinse and drain, then continue as per recipe.

Heat 30 ml olive oil in a deep saucepan. Add the onion and sauté until softened, about 10 minutes. Add the celery and carrots and cook for another 5 minutes. Stir in the garlic, ginger and lemon zest, and cook for 1–2 minutes.

Add all the spices, tomato paste, tomatoes, lentils, sorghum and stock. Bring the soup up to the boil, then cover with a lid and simmer for 20 minutes. Stir in the quinoa and simmer for a further 20 minutes. Add the chickpeas and lemon juice, and heat through.

FOR THE SALSA, combine all the ingredients in a bowl and chill until needed. Serve the salsa alongside the soup.

GINGERY CHICKPEA CURRY WITH ROAST HARISSA AUBERGINES

If you're looking to include more plant-based meals into everyday cooking, a vegetable curry is an excellent place to start. It marries pantry staples – chickpeas and butter beans – with a handful of dried spices to create a wholesome and satisfying supper. I've included roast aubergine, as an optional extra, which is a little more work, but can be done in the same time as it takes to cook the curry.

SERVES 4–6

- olive oil, for cooking
- 1 red onion, finely diced
- 1 clove garlic, minced
- 4 cm piece of ginger, freshly grated
- 5 ml ground cumin or 7.5 ml cumin seeds
- 10 ml ground coriander
- 5 ml ground turmeric
- 2.5 ml dried red chilli flakes
- 1 x 400 g tin chopped tomatoes
- 375 ml vegetable stock
- 1 x 400 g tin coconut milk
- 3 bay leaves
- 2 x 400 g tins chickpeas, rinsed and drained
- 1 x 400 g tin butter beans, rinsed and drained
- fine salt and freshly ground black pepper

Heat 30 ml olive oil in a deep saucepan and sauté the onion until soft, about 10 minutes. Add the garlic and ginger, and cook for another minute or two. Add all the dry spices, including the chilli, and mix to coat the onion. At this point, the onion will look dry and rubbly.

Add the tomatoes, stock, coconut milk and bay leaves. Stir gently and bring up to the boil. Cover with a lid and simmer for 30 minutes. Add the chickpeas and butter beans, then cook for a further 10 minutes. Season to taste.

Serve with basmati rice, yoghurt and Peanut & Mint Salsa. Alternately, add the Roast Harissa Aubergines and a scattering of dukkah, to finish.

PEANUT & MINT SALSA Combine 50 g roughly chopped salted peanuts, 1 finely sliced red chilli, a handful each of roughly chopped fresh mint, parsley and fennel, 15 ml lemon juice, 45 ml olive oil, a pinch of fine salt and freshly ground black pepper.

ROAST HARISSA AUBERGINES Preheat the oven to 200°C. Place 2 aubergines (cut into chunks) in a roasting tin. Drizzle with olive oil and season with fine salt and freshly ground black pepper. Roast for 30 minutes. In a bowl, combine 15 ml harissa paste, 22.5 ml olive oil, 15 ml sesame seeds and 10 ml honey. Brush the harissa marinade over the aubergines and toss to coat. Roast for a further 5 minutes. Sprinkle with dukkah to finish.

SPICY LENTIL-STUFFED AUBERGINE WITH SOY & HONEY TAHINI SAUCE

I'm often asked what makes a good vegetarian main. This is it. Roasting lentils may sound like a complete waste of time, but once roasted, these lens-shaped seeds shift from bland to robust in both texture and flavour. It gives meat a run for its money.

SERVES 8–10

olive oil, for roasting
4 medium aubergines, halved, flesh scored diagonally
fine salt and freshly ground black pepper

ROAST LENTILS
15 ml olive oil
1 x 400 g tin lentils, rinsed, drained and blotted on paper towel
5 ml ground cumin
2.5 ml ground turmeric
2.5 ml dried red chilli flakes
fine salt and freshly ground black pepper

FILLING
olive oil, for cooking
1 large brown onion, finely diced
1 clove garlic, minced
5 ml ground coriander
10 ml ground cumin
7.5 ml paprika
5 ml dried oregano
15 ml tomato paste
1 x 400 g tin chopped tomatoes
350 ml vegetable stock
5 ml sugar
1 x quantity Roast Lentils (*see* opposite)
a generous handful of fresh mint and flat-leaf parsley, roughly chopped, plus extra to finish
100 g feta
extra virgin olive oil, to drizzle
toasted sesame seeds, to finish

SOY & HONEY TAHINI SAUCE
60 ml tahini
80 ml water
15 ml soy sauce
30 ml lemon juice
10 ml honey
10 ml sesame oil
1.25 ml black pepper

START WITH THE LENTILS. Preheat the oven to 220°C. Line a large roasting tin with baking paper.

Drizzle 15 ml olive oil over the lentils and season with cumin, turmeric, chilli, salt and pepper. Toss to coat, then arrange to one side of the roasting tin.

Brush the cut side of the aubergines liberally with olive oil, and season with salt and black pepper. Arrange, cut side down, alongside the lentils. Roast for 30 minutes, stirring the lentils halfway through the cooking time.

IN THE MEANTIME, MAKE THE FILLING. Heat 15 ml olive oil in a saucepan. Add the onion and sauté over medium heat until softened, about 10 minutes. Stir through the garlic and cook for another minute or two. Add all the dried spices and tomato paste, and cook for 2 minutes. Add the tomatoes, stock and sugar. Cover and simmer for 15 minutes. Stir in the roast lentils and cook for another 5 minutes, then add the mint and parsley.

Turn the aubergines over and press the softened flesh down to create hollows. Fill with the lentil mixture. Crumble over the feta and drizzle lightly with olive oil. Roast for a further 20 minutes until bubbling and golden.

FOR THE SOY & HONEY TAHINI SAUCE, place all the ingredients in a small mixing bowl and whisk until smooth.

Drizzle half the tahini sauce over the aubergines and scatter with sesame seeds. Offer the remaining sauce alongside.

CHICKEN & CHORIZO RIGATONI

I cooked this pasta dish for a well-known Italian restaurant some years back. It was so popular that they put it on their menu. It remains our most-loved pasta to date. Caution is advisable when using saffron. A judicious pinch is all it needs.

SERVES 4–6

olive oil, for cooking
500 g chicken thighs, skinless and deboned, cut into strips
fine salt and freshly ground black pepper
100 g chorizo, thinly sliced
125 ml white wine (chenin blanc)
1 x quantity Roast Cherry Tomato & Red Pepper Sauce (*see* below)
a pinch of saffron, soaked in 15 ml hot water
zest of ½ lemon
125 ml water
400 g rigatoni pasta
freshly grated parmesan, to serve
Simple Pangrattato (page 124), to finish (optional)

ROAST CHERRY TOMATO & RED PEPPER SAUCE

1 kg cherry tomatoes, halved
2 red sweet peppers, deseeded and roughly chopped
2 red onions, cut into wedges
3 cloves garlic
olive oil, for roasting
10 ml herbes de Provence
10 ml dried oregano
3.75 ml dried red chilli flakes
5 ml fine salt
freshly ground black pepper
5 sprigs of fresh thyme
6 sundried tomatoes in oil
2.5 ml sugar
50 g grated parmesan
550 ml vegetable stock

FIRST MAKE THE SAUCE. Preheat the oven to 200°C. Arrange the tomatoes, sweet peppers, onion and garlic in a large roasting tin. Drizzle over 30–45 ml olive oil. Add the dried herbs and chilli and season well with salt and black pepper. Toss to coat, then tuck the thyme under the vegetables. Roast for 55–60 minutes.

Remove the thyme stalks before scraping everything into a blender. Add the sundried tomatoes, sugar, parmesan and stock. You may need to do this in two batches. Blitz until smooth.

Heat 15 ml olive oil in a wide-based pan. Season the chicken with salt and pepper. Cook over a high heat until golden on all sides. Move the chicken to one side of the pan. Add the chorizo and cook for several minutes, until the fat renders. Deglaze the pan with the wine and reduce by half.

Add half the roast tomato sauce, saffron, lemon zest and water. Simmer on low for 12–15 minutes.

Cook the pasta in plenty of well-salted, boiling water. Reserve 250 ml of the cooking water before draining. Add the pasta to the sauce and toss to coat. Use the reserved pasta water – in part or full – to loosen the sauce.

Serve with plenty of grated parmesan and pangrattato.

COOK'S NOTE: The Roast Cherry Tomato & Red Pepper Sauce recipe makes enough for two dinners. Use half the quantity for the Chicken & Chorizo Rigatoni and freeze the remainder for later.

SPINACH & WALNUT PESTO BUCATINI

We are never without some kind of pesto in the fridge. This one is crammed with good things, so I make it often.

SERVES 4–6

400 g bucatini pasta
150 g garden peas
freshly grated parmesan, to finish
black pepper, to finish
extra virgin olive oil, to drizzle

SPINACH & WALNUT PESTO
MAKES 500 ML

70 g walnuts, toasted
30 g almonds, toasted
100 g baby spinach
40 g fresh basil
40 g rocket
2 cloves garlic
40 g parmesan, grated
zest of 1 lemon
30 ml lemon juice
fine salt and freshly ground black pepper
125 ml extra virgin olive oil, plus extra to finish

FIRST MAKE THE PESTO. Place the walnuts and almonds in a food processor. Pulse until broken down. Add all the remaining ingredients, except the oil, and blend until the pesto is smooth. Add the olive oil and stir through to combine. Spoon into a sterilized jar.

Bring a large pot of salted water to the boil. Cook the pasta until al dente. Reserve about 300 ml of the cooking water before draining.

Return the pot to the heat, add half the pesto (250 ml) and the peas, and heat through. Add the pasta and as much of the reserved water to create a sauce.

Serve immediately with plenty of parmesan, black pepper and a drizzle of olive oil.

SPELT PIZZA WITH SPINACH & WALNUT PESTO & CRISPY KALE

In the end, a really good pizza comes down to the crust. The sauce and toppings are made to order. In Naples, the Margherita is queen, while in the US, pepperoni leaves its competitors in the dust, which begs the question, what's with the green pizza? I'm sure if I set up shop in Naples, selling wholemeal kale pizzas, I'd be hung in the piazza at dawn. In the meantime, I'll keep making them. They are absolutely scrumptious with heaps of wholesomeness. If you want to side with the Italians, which we often do, ladle over a spoon of the Roast Cherry Tomato and Red Pepper Sauce (page 149), top with mozzarella and thinly sliced pepperoni, or spicy salami. *Delicioso!*

MAKES 2

DOUGH
150 g Tipo 00 flour
100 g wholegrain spelt flour
3.75 ml fine salt
5 ml instant dry yeast
160–170 ml water, tepid temperature
15 ml olive oil
semolina, for rolling

TOPPING
60 ml Spinach & Walnut Pesto (page 150)
½ bunch curly kale, centre rib removed, and roughly torn
4–5 medium baby marrows, shaved into lengths
extra virgin olive oil, to drizzle
fine salt and freshly ground black pepper
150 g fior di latte or mozzarella, torn
toasted pumpkin and sunflower seeds
grated parmesan, to finish
fresh basil sprigs

TO MAKE THE DOUGH, place all the ingredients, except the semolina, in the bowl of an electric mixer. With the dough hook attached, mix to combine. Knead on a low speed until smooth, 6–8 minutes. Transfer the dough to an oiled bowl, cover with cling film and set aside to proof until doubled.

Divide the dough in half, cover with a tea towel and rest for 15 minutes.

Preheat the oven to 250°C. Place a pizza stone or baking sheet in the oven while heating.

Dust the work surface lightly with a little flour and semolina. Roll the dough out to a thickness of 3 mm. Divide the pesto between each and spread evenly, leaving a 2 cm border.

Place the kale and baby marrow in a large mixing bowl. Drizzle over 22.5 ml olive oil and season lightly with salt and black pepper. Pile the vegetables onto the pizza bases and top with the fior di latte or mozzarella.

Bake until golden, about 15 minutes. Scatter over the toasted seeds and parmesan. Finish with fresh basil and a good olive oil. Serve immediately.

RED THAI GOCHUJANG SALMON CURRY

Our weeknight curry relies on a good store-bought paste and gochujang, a spicy fermented paste popular in Korean cooking. Lemongrass, ginger and garlic add pungency and contrast to the richness of coconut milk and peanut butter.

Swap the salmon for chicken – thighs or fillets – if you prefer. While the flavours are complex, the recipe is a cinch.

SERVES 4

- coconut oil, for cooking
- 4 x 125 g salmon fillets
- 2.5 ml each of ground coriander, cumin and paprika
- fine salt
- 2 shallots, finely diced
- 2 cloves garlic, minced
- 15 ml freshly grated ginger
- 1 stalk lemongrass, outer layer removed and discarded, finely diced
- 30 ml Thai red curry paste
- 45 ml peanut butter
- 10 ml gochujang paste
- 45 ml soy sauce
- 22.5 ml lime juice
- 30 ml fish sauce
- 15 ml brown sugar
- 1 x 400 g tin coconut milk
- 250 ml chicken stock
- steamed basmati rice, to serve
- spring onions, thinly sliced, to serve

Heat 15 ml coconut oil in a non-stick pan. Season the salmon on both sides with coriander, cumin, paprika and salt. Lay the salmon, skin side down, in the pan and cook for about 4 minutes. Turn and cook for a further 3 minutes, or to your liking. Remove to a plate and cover while you make the sauce.

In the same pan, sauté the shallots until softened, about 6 minutes. Add the garlic, ginger and lemongrass, and cook for 2 minutes. Stir in the curry paste, peanut butter and gochujang paste, and cook for another minute or two.

Add the soy sauce, lime juice, fish sauce and sugar. Pour in the coconut milk and stock, then bring up to the boil. Simmer until reduced and thickened, around 15 minutes should do.

Lay the salmon in the sauce and heat through gently.

Serve with basmati rice, thinly sliced spring onions and toppings of your choice (roughly chopped roasted and salted peanuts, pickled red onion, fresh coriander). Offer with Gochujang Drizzle, if you like.

GOCHUJANG DRIZZLE Combine 5 ml gochujang paste, 10 ml sesame oil, 10 ml lemon juice, 5 ml honey and a pinch of Maldon sea salt flakes. Drizzle over the salmon just before serving.

WEEKNIGHT TUSCAN CHICKEN

You'd be hard pressed to find this recipe on a Tuscan menu, but it does a fine job of conjuring up a romanticized taste of Italy. There's rosemary, parmesan and sundried tomatoes. How can it not be good? Every time I make this dish, the pan hardly needs rinsing.

SERVES 4

4 free-range, skinless chicken fillets
5 ml herbes de Provence
2 sprigs of fresh rosemary, leaves picked and finely chopped
fine salt and freshly ground black pepper
olive oil, for cooking
1 large shallot, finely diced
1–2 cloves garlic, minced
zest of 1 lemon
6–8 sundried tomatoes in olive oil, thinly sliced
60 ml white wine (chenin blanc)
80 ml chicken stock
125 ml fresh cream
5 ml cornflour whisked with 30 ml milk
25 g parmesan, freshly grated
several lemon slices, to finish

Place the chicken between two sheets of baking paper and pound lightly to flatten and tenderize. Season on both sides with the herbes, rosemary, salt and pepper.

Heat 15 ml olive oil in a wide-based pan. Place the chicken in the hot oil and cook without turning, until golden – about 5 minutes. Turn and cook for a further 4 minutes. Remove the chicken and set aside.

Add a little more oil to the pan and sauté the shallots until softened, 6–8 minutes. Add the garlic, lemon zest and sundried tomatoes, and cook for about 2 minutes.

Deglaze with the wine, scraping up all the sticky bits, and reduce slightly. Stir in the stock, cream and cornflour slurry. Bring up to a simmer, then add the parmesan and stir through. Nestle the chicken in the sauce and simmer until reduced and thickened, around 3–4 minutes should do.

Add lemon slices and serve immediately with pan-grilled broccolini, mashed potatoes, pasta, polenta or steamed green beans. Crusty bread is especially good.

FENNEL CHICKEN MEATBALLS WITH BUTTER BEAN MASH

I've made these with pork mince, too. Both options are a good match with fennel. Wetting your hands with cold water will help when rolling the mixture into balls.

SERVES 4

1 shallot, finely diced
2 small or 1 medium fennel bulb, core removed, and finely diced (125 ml loosely packed)
olive oil, for cooking and drizzling
1 clove garlic, minced
2 baby marrows, coarsely grated
3.75 ml fine salt
500 g chicken mince
150 g fresh breadcrumbs
zest of 1 lemon
a generous handful of fresh flat-leaf parsley, roughly chopped
freshly ground black pepper
1 x quantity Quick Butter Bean Mash with Dill Salsa (page 116)
sprigs of fresh fennel, to finish
fresh basil leaves, to finish

Start by sautéing the shallot and fennel in 15 ml olive oil until softened, around 8 minutes. Add the garlic and baby marrows and cook for several minutes or until all the moisture has evaporated. Season lightly with salt, then set aside to cool.

Place all the meatball ingredients, up to and including the black pepper, in a bowl. Add the cooled shallots and fennel, and mix to combine. Roll into balls, cover and chill for at least 30 minutes.

Meanwhile, make the butter bean mash and dill salsa according to the instructions.

Heat 15 ml olive oil in a pan. Fry the meatballs until golden on all sides and cooked through. Add a splash of water to deglaze and lift the sticky bits off the base of the pan.

Spread the butter bean mash on a serving plate. Place the meatballs on top and finish with the dill salsa.

EASY BUTTER CHICKEN CURRY WITH BROWNED BUTTER

A breeze to put together once you've made the curry paste. Spicy but not overly hot. Drizzle over the hot, browned butter at the end and let it trickle into the sauce.

SERVES 4

700 g skinless chicken fillets, cut into large cubes
160 ml Butter Chicken Curry Paste (page 38), divided
fine salt and freshly ground black pepper
vegetable oil, for cooking
1 x 400 g tin chopped tomatoes
180 ml chicken stock (250 ml for a thinner sauce)
5 ml brown sugar
1 cinnamon stick
250 ml Greek or double-cream yoghurt
40 g butter (optional)

Place the chicken and 80 ml curry paste in a non-metallic bowl. Season lightly with salt and black pepper, and toss to coat. Cover and set aside to marinate for 30 minutes or overnight, if time allows.

Heat 15 ml oil in a wide-based pan until hot. Cook the chicken for several minutes, more to sear than brown. Scrape in the remaining paste and cook for 2–3 minutes. Add the tomatoes, stock, sugar and cinnamon stick. Cover partially and simmer for 15 minutes. Stir through the yoghurt and cook for a further 10 minutes.

For the browned butter, heat the butter in a small saucepan over a medium heat. Once the butter is melted, turn the heat up and let it splutter away until nutty and golden in colour.

Pour the hot, browned butter over the curry just before serving and swirl through. Offer with warm naan bread, steamed basmati rice and Quick Herb Yoghurt (*see* below), if you like.

QUICK HERB YOGHURT Combine 125 ml Greek yoghurt with the zest of 1 lemon, 15 ml lemon juice, a pinch of fine salt, and a handful of finely chopped fresh mint, coriander and flat-leaf parsley.

HARISSA & SUMAC CHICKEN KEBABS

Grilled over coals, the chicken becomes charred and smoky, although midweek, a griddled pan will get the job done in minutes. Do remember to keep an eye on the kebabs, turning regularly as the sugars in the marinade burn easily. Double the quantity of harissa in the marinade if you want more intensity.

SERVES 6

olive oil, for cooking
700 g skinless and deboned chicken thighs, cut in half lengthways
lemon cheeks, to serve (optional)

MARINADE
15 ml harissa paste
5 ml sumac
5 ml dried oregano
2.5 ml paprika
5 ml honey or pomegranate molasses
zest of 1 lemon
15 ml lemon juice
30 ml olive oil
2.5 ml Maldon sea salt flakes

YOGHURT SAUCE
125 ml Greek yoghurt
2.5 ml sumac

FOR THE MARINADE, combine all the ingredients in a non-metallic bowl. Add the chicken pieces and toss to coat. Cover with cling film and set aside to marinate for at least 30 minutes, or overnight. Thread two to three pieces onto each skewer.

Heat 15 ml olive oil in a wide-based pan until hot. Cook the chicken for several minutes per side until slightly charred around the edges and cooked through. Add a splash of water to deglaze the pan and lift all the marmite-y goodness.

FOR THE SAUCE, combine the yoghurt and sumac in a small bowl.

Serve the kebabs with the sauce and lemon cheeks.

GOAN MINCE & POTATO PASTRIES

Tamarind or vinegar, for souring, is commonplace in Goan cooking. If using tamarind, go sparingly. It can be puckeringly tart.

Swaddled in flaky pastry, it takes curry in a new direction. To make it midweek friendly, forgo the pastry and serve with steamed basmati rice and a cooling raita.

MAKES 4

2 x 400 g ready-made puff pastry
egg wash (1 egg whisked with 15 ml water)
black and white sesame seeds and cumin seeds, to finish

FILLING
vegetable or coconut oil, for cooking
1 large red onion, finely diced
2 cloves garlic, minced
15 ml freshly grated ginger
500 g lean beef mince
10 ml garam masala
5 ml ground coriander
5 ml paprika
2.5 ml ground turmeric
5 ml red chilli flakes
fine salt and freshly ground black pepper
15 ml tomato paste
1 x 400 g tin chopped tomatoes
5 ml sugar
250 ml chicken stock
15 ml apple cider vinegar or 5 ml tamarind paste, dissolved in 30 ml hot water
2 medium potatoes, peeled and cut into 1 cm dice
fine salt and freshly ground black pepper

FIRST MAKE THE FILLING. Heat 15 ml oil in a deep saucepan. Add the onion and sauté over a medium heat until softened, about 10 minutes. Stir in the garlic and ginger and cook for another minute.

Add the mince and brown over a high heat, breaking it up with a wooden spoon. Add all the dried spices up to and including the chilli. Season with salt and black pepper. Continue cooking the meat until it is deeply caramelized and the base of the pan sounds dry and scratchy.

Stir in the tomato paste, tomatoes, sugar, stock, and vinegar or tamarind. Add the potatoes and bring up to a simmer. Cover partially and cook for about 40 minutes. The sauce should be well reduced but not dry. Set aside to cool.

Preheat the oven to 200°C.

Lightly roll out each sheet of pastry on a floured board and cut in half lengthways. You will have four rectangular pieces, each measuring 30 x 12 cm. Divide the mince equally and place it down the centre of each pastry sheet, leaving a 5 cm border on each side. Cut 2 cm strips on either side of the mince. Plait the pastry strips from top to bottom, pinching the ends to seal.

Transfer to a lined baking sheet. Brush with egg wash and scatter over the sesame seeds and cumin seeds. Bake for 40–45 minutes or until golden. Serve with Mrs Ball's Chutney or the Pear & Sultana Chutney (page 207).

SAFFRON & HONEY ROAST LAMB WITH PRESERVED LEMON & DATES

Lamb is gorgeously grand, evoking a real sense of occasion. Here, the sharp acidity of preserved lemon cuts through the lamb's goodly layer of fat. As with most sizeable cuts of meat, overnight marinating does wonders to deepen the flavours.

SERVES 8–10

- 2.5 kg free-range leg of lamb
- 3 red onions, peeled and sliced into wedges
- ½ garlic bulb
- olive oil, for roasting
- Maldon sea salt flakes and freshly ground black pepper
- 125 ml chicken stock
- 180 ml white wine
- 45 ml lemon juice
- 8 Medjool dates, pitted and halved
- griddled lemon halves, to serve

SAFFRON & HONEY MARINADE

- 45 ml olive oil
- 45 ml honey
- 15 ml lemon juice
- ¼ preserved lemon (skin only), mulched into a paste
- 2 cloves garlic, finely minced
- 10 ml cumin seeds
- 2.5 ml fennel seeds
- 10 ml ground coriander
- 5 ml dried red chilli flakes
- a pinch of saffron threads, steeped in 10 ml hot water
- 7.5 ml Maldon sea salt flakes
- freshly ground black pepper

FIRST MAKE THE MARINADE. Place all the ingredients in a small mixing bowl and stir to combine.

Rub the marinade into the lamb, making sure the entire surface is covered. Place in a non-metallic dish, cover and chill overnight. I turn the meat over once during the marinating period. Before roasting, bring the meat up to room temperature.

Preheat the oven to 180°C. Arrange the onions and garlic in a large roasting tin. Drizzle over 30 ml olive oil, and season lightly with salt and black pepper. Sprinkle a little more salt over the lamb and place it on top of the onions, fatty side facing down.

Add the stock to the roasting tin, cover with foil and roast for 2½ hours.

Remove the foil and turn the lamb over, fatty side up. Add the wine, lemon juice and dates. Roast for 60 minutes uncovered, basting with the pan juices after 30 minutes. To render the fat, increase the oven temperature to 220°C and roast for 15 minutes until deeply caramelized.

Serve with griddled lemon halves.

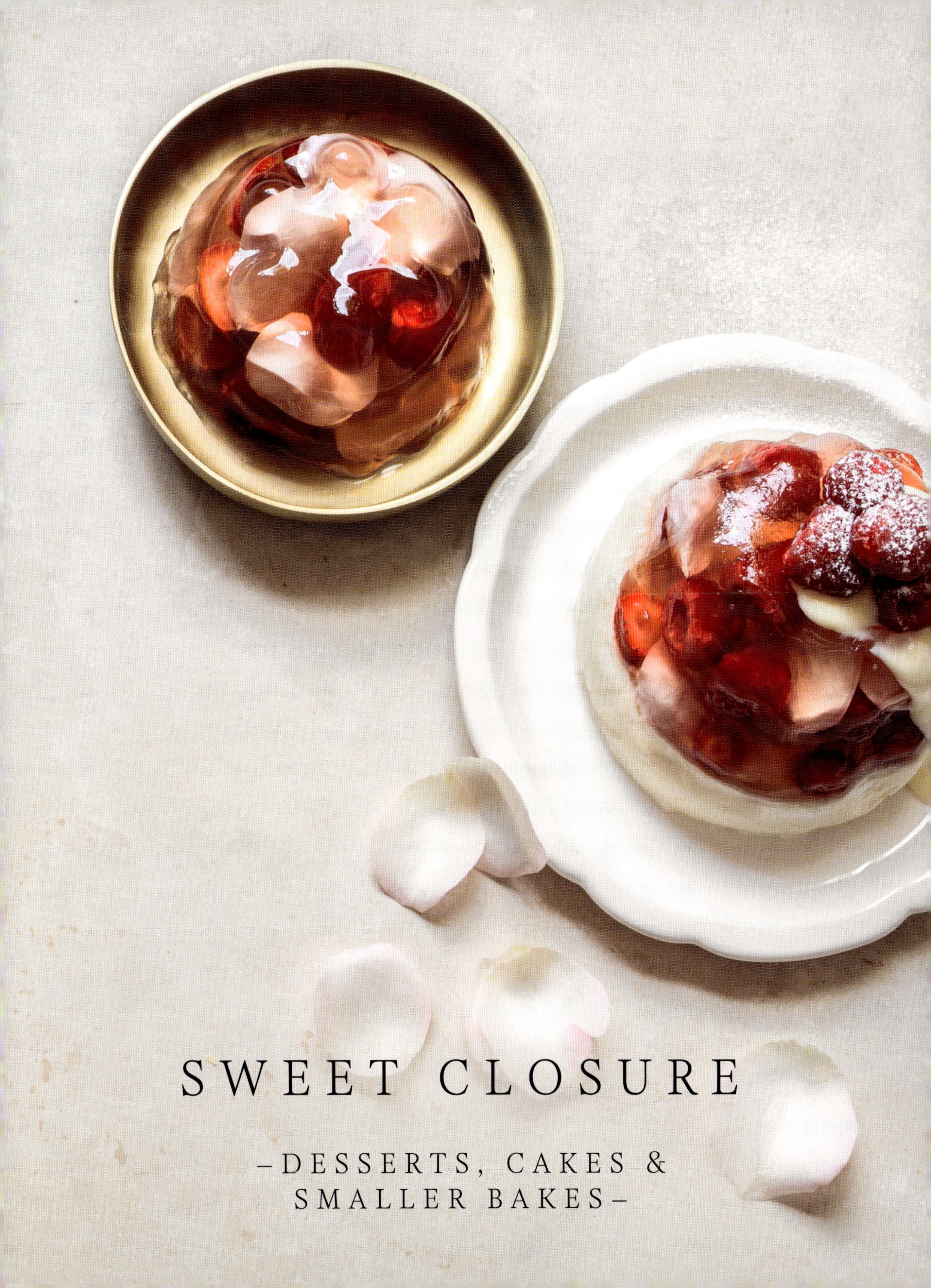

SWEET CLOSURE

–DESSERTS, CAKES & SMALLER BAKES–

No longer are there hard and fast rules when it comes to dessert or when we should be enjoying it. With this in mind, many of the recipes in our sweet chapter pendulum effortlessly between dessert, afternoon tea and in-between treat.

Make-ahead desserts come with a slew of hidden benefits, leaving nothing to chance, just on-the-money success. When you need impressive without the risk of failure, these are the recipes to pull out of your back pocket. The Burnt Basque Cheesecake (page 186), Sicilian Orange Torte (page 188) and Panna Cotta (page 176) are dinner-party perfect, and can be prepared in advance. Strangely enough, the torte develops a more intense, concentrated orange flavour the longer it sits, while the Basque cheesecake defies all the rules of cheesecake making – whisked together in a blender, nonetheless. It'll sweep 'em off their feet.

For serious chocolate lovers, the no-bake Leopard Chocolate Biscuit Cake (page 191) ticks all the boxes. Besides ease and convenience – a bit of chopping and chocolate melting – its lifespan can, but in all likelihood won't, stretch to two digits. Of course it's rich, almost fudgy, the intensity dialled back to a degree by chunky bits of biscuit and tart cranberries. Immensely good washed down with an espresso.

BAKING NOTES

- Baking times and temperatures are based on conventional ovens.
- Always test for doneness with a skewer while the bake is still in the oven. If not quite done, extend the baking time in 5-minute increments, or until the skewer comes out clean.
- Eggs are extra large
- Butter is salted
- Olive oil is extra virgin
- Replace alcohol with a slightly acidic equivalent – pomegranate molasses, balsamic vinegar or fresh orange juice.

LIME CURD MASCARPONE CREAM TARTS

Some years back, I asked Darren what cake he'd like for his birthday. He replied he doesn't really like cake. Maybe a lemon meringue pie. Pie isn't cake, is it? And who doesn't like cake? Disappointed, I relented and made the lemon meringue. In this simplified version, lime curd delivers the necessary tang, while mascarpone curbs the sweetness. I've also moved on from the cake affair.

MAKES 6

CRUST
200 g Bakers Tennis Biscuits
15 ml icing sugar
90 g butter, melted

FILLING
250 g mascarpone
250 ml Lime Curd (page 32)

MERINGUE
2 egg whites
100 g castor sugar
a pinch of fine salt

FOR THE CRUST, place the biscuits and icing sugar in a processor. Pulse at 20-second intervals until the texture is fine. Drizzle in the butter and blitz to combine.

Divide the mixture between 6 loose-bottomed tart tins (8 cm width) and press to line the base and sides. Chill for 30 minutes.

FOR THE FILLING, scrape the mascarpone into a mixing bowl. Using a metal spoon, mix the mascarpone gently to loosen. Add the lime curd and stir gently to combine. Once the curd is added, it's safe to use a balloon whisk. Whisk until smooth. Spoon the filling into the pastry cases and chill for several hours or overnight.

TO MAKE THE MERINGUE, place the egg whites, sugar and salt in a bowl set over a pan of simmering water. Cook for 5–7 minutes, whisking constantly, until the sugar is dissolved and the mixture frothy.

Transfer the egg whites to a mixer and whisk until the meringue peaks and holds its shape.

Gently unmould the tarts and place on a serving plate. Dollop a spoonful of meringue onto each tart, or use a piping bag. Scorch with a blowtorch just before serving.

Keeps well in the fridge for 2 days.

COOK'S NOTE: In place of individual moulds, use a 20 cm tart tin.

HONEY BUTTER NECTARINES

Nuanced with bittersweet complexity, every mouthful a swoop of summer. Gloriously simple.

Not to be mistaken for chewy-centred amaretti, cookie snaps are crunchy and darker in colour, with a bitter edge. You'll find them at your favourite Italian deli and select supermarkets.

SERVES 4–6

30 ml butter, melted
22.5 ml light muscovado sugar
30 ml honey
1.25 ml ground mixed spice
4 nectarines, ripe but firm, halved and pitted
15 ml lemon juice
30 ml bourbon or orange juice
60 ml water

TO FINISH
Amaretti cookie snaps
vanilla bean ice cream (optional)

To the melted butter, add the sugar, honey and mixed spice. Brush half the honey butter onto the cut side of the fruit.

Heat a non-stick pan until hot. Place the fruit, cut side down in the pan and cook until caramelized, 3–4 minutes. Turn, then brush with the remaining honey butter. Cook for several minutes, then turn once more.

Add the lemon juice and bourbon or orange juice, and swish the pan around to lift the sticky bits. Immediately add the water and reduce until the sauce is glossy.

Crush 2 or 3 amaretti onto each plate. Arrange the nectarines on top and drizzle over the pan juices. Finish with a scoop of vanilla bean ice cream. Serve straight away.

COCONUT PANNA COTTA & GRANADILLA DUO

The sign of a good panna cotta is its delicate quiver and silk-like viscosity.

Your spoon should glide through the wobbly cream. Do use fresh granadilla pulp rather than tinned. The tang needs to be bright and lively, a necessary contrast to the sweetened cream.

SERVES 8–10

JELLY
15 ml gelatine powder
500 ml granadilla juice
125 ml fresh granadilla pulp
30 ml lemon juice
50 g castor sugar

PANNA COTTA
15 ml gelatine powder
250 ml coconut milk
250 ml fresh cream
100 g castor sugar
1 vanilla pod, split and seeds scraped

TO FINISH
125 ml fresh cream
fresh pulp of 2–3 granadillas

FOR THE JELLY, sponge the gelatine in 30 ml cold water.

Place the granadilla juice and pulp, lemon juice and castor sugar in a saucepan. Stir over a medium heat until the sugar is dissolved.

Heat the gelatine until dissolved, then add to the warm juice. Whisk well to combine. Pour into a large ring mould or individual pudding moulds. Chill until just set.

FOR THE PANNA COTTA, sponge the gelatine in 30 ml cold water.

In a saucepan, heat the coconut milk, cream, castor sugar and vanilla seeds, stirring all the while. Once tiny bubbles break the surface, remove from the heat.

Heat the gelatine until dissolved, then add to the cream mixture and whisk to combine. Set aside to cool completely. Pour the cream carefully over the set jelly and refrigerate for 3 hours or until set.

To unmould, dip briefly in hot water and invert onto a serving plate. Drizzle with fresh cream and granadilla pulp.

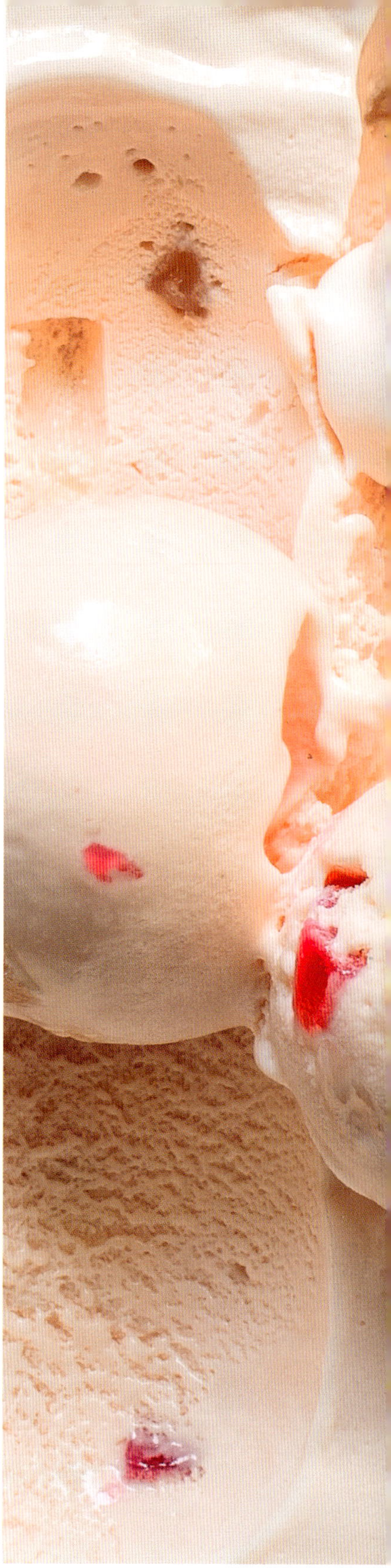

CHEEKY CHEAT'S ICE CREAM

Once you've made proper ice cream, you're ruined. But, if the ship is sinking and you're struggling to keep afloat, trickery can save the day. When I need to cheat, here's what I do.

MAKES ABOUT 1.8 LITRES

TURKISH DELIGHT ICE CREAM
15 ml rosewater (not extract)
a few drops of pink food colouring
2 litres vanilla ice cream, softened
200 g soft Turkish delight, cut into small dice

GINGERBREAD PUDDING ICE CREAM
5 ml ground cinnamon
1.25 ml ground mixed spice
2 litres vanilla ice cream, softened
150 g ginger biscuits, roughly chopped
30 ml finely diced preserved ginger
30 ml preserved ginger syrup, to drizzle

BLUEBERRY RIPPLE ICE CREAM
½ x quantity Quick Blueberry Compote (page 80)
2 litres vanilla ice cream, softened

FOR THE TURKISH DELIGHT, add the rosewater and colouring to the ice cream. Mix well, then fold through the Turkish delight.

FOR THE GINGERBREAD PUDDING, mix the spices into the ice cream, then fold through the biscuit chunks and ginger pieces. Drizzle with syrup before serving.

FOR THE BLUEBERRY RIPPLE, make the compote according to the method on page 80 and fold it through the softened ice cream, without overmixing. The ice cream should be streaked.

Once the flavourings have been added, transfer the ice creams to their respective containers and freeze until firm.

ROSÉ & RASPBERRY JELLY

22.5 ml gelatine powder
1 x 750 ml bottle of
Babylonstoren Rosé
170 g castor sugar
30 ml lemon juice
375 ml fresh raspberries
and strawberries
a handful of fresh, unsprayed
rose petals (optional)

Sponge the gelatine in 30 ml cold water.

Place the wine, castor sugar and lemon juice in a saucepan. Stir over a medium heat until the sugar is dissolved.

Heat the gelatine until dissolved, then add to the warm liquid. Whisk well to combine. Allow to cool, then stir in the fruit and petals, if using. Pour into a large ring mould or individual pudding moulds, and chill until just set.

RASPBERRY MILLE FEUILLE

Crème diplomate, a baker's classic, is essentially crème pâtissière with the addition of whipped cream and, in some instances, gelatine to help stabilize its structure. Perfect for filling choux buns, layered cakes and tarts.

SERVES 12

2 x quantity Brown Butter Buckwheat Crêpes (page 80)
400 g raspberries
icing sugar, to finish

CRÈME DIPLOMATE
500 ml full-cream milk, plus 30 ml extra
2 eggs
90 g castor sugar
30 ml cornflour
30 ml cake wheat flour
a pinch of fine salt
10 ml vanilla paste or extract
5 ml gelatine powder
500 ml whipping cream
30 ml icing sugar

First make the crêpes according to the method on page 80.

FOR THE CRÈME DIPLOMATE, place the 500 ml milk in a saucepan over a medium heat and bring up to the boil.

In a heatproof bowl, whisk together the eggs, castor sugar, cornflour, cake wheat flour, salt and the 30 ml milk.

Add the hot milk to the egg mixture in a steady stream, whisking all the while. Pour the mixture back into the pan and cook over a medium heat until thickened, whisking continuously. Simmer gently for several minutes to remove any floury taste. Stir in the vanilla paste or extract.

Sponge the gelatine in 15 ml cold water for several minutes. Warm to dissolve, then add to the custard. Whisk well to combine. Strain into a clean bowl. Press a layer of cling film directly onto the surface to prevent a skin forming. Cool on the counter, then chill until needed.

Whisk the cream and icing sugar together until soft peak stage.

Remove the custard from the fridge and whisk lightly to loosen. Add the whipped cream and fold through.

TO ASSEMBLE, place the first pancake on a cake stand. Spread with 30 ml crème diplomate. Repeat the layering until all the pancakes and filling are used up. Top with raspberries and dust with icing sugar just before serving.

WALNUT & DATE MA'AMOUL

Nicky, at your insistence, and because your husband said they were the best ma'amoul he's ever had! A fair bit of work goes into these distinctive cookies, but the reward is tenfold. Ma'amoul, meaning 'filled', are found throughout the Middle East. You can shape and fashion them by hand, or use a traditional wooden mould.

MAKES 18

SPICED DUSTING SUGAR
45 ml icing sugar
1.25 ml ground cinnamon
a pinch of ground mixed spice

DOUGH
160 g cake wheat flour
100 g fine semolina
25 g icing sugar
2 cardamom pods, crushed, husks removed, and finely ground
a pinch of fine salt
a pinch of baking powder
125 g salted butter, melted
45 ml full-cream milk, slightly warm

WALNUT & DATE FILLING
100 g walnuts, toasted
140 g Medjool dates, pitted and chopped
zest of 1 orange
2.5 ml ground cinnamon
1.25 ml ground nutmeg
10 ml olive oil

FIRST MAKE THE DUSTING SUGAR by sifting together the icing sugar, cinnamon and mixed spice.

FOR THE DOUGH, sift together the cake wheat flour, semolina, icing sugar, cardamom, salt and baking powder in a mixing bowl.

Whisk together the butter and milk, then add to the dry ingredients. Mix to combine – I use a wooden spoon here. Wrap the dough in cling film and chill for 45 minutes.

FOR THE FILLING, place the nuts in a processor and blitz until rubbly, but not too fine. Add the dates, orange zest, spices and olive oil. Blitz until the mixture balls together. Roll teaspoon amounts of the date mixture into balls – it should yield around 18.

Preheat the oven to 180°C. Line a large baking sheet with baking paper.

Pinch off tablespoon amounts of dough (25 g each) and roll into balls. Press or roll into discs, about 8 cm in width. Place a date ball in the centre of each, folding the edges inward and pinching together to seal.

Roll gently to smooth, then place in a ma'amoul mould. Press down firmly. Tap on the counter to release, then place on the baking sheet. Repeat with the remaining dough and filling.

Bake for 22 minutes. Turn the baking sheet around, increase the oven temperature to 190°C and bake for a further 5 minutes.

Transfer to a wire rack to cool. Once cooled, dust generously with the dusting sugar.

Store in an airtight container for 5–7 days.

COOK'S NOTE: Brush the ma'amoul mould lightly with olive oil before use.

BURNT BASQUE CHEESECAKE WITH ALMOND COOKIE CRUST

Burnished, and I mean one shade short of blackened, with a buttery soft belly. Queen of cheesecakes, the Basque poufs up like a soufflé before caving into comfortability. I've added an almond biscuit crust with a knife point of mixed spice, both commonplace in Spanish desserts, but not traditional to a Basque. Treasonable, I suppose, but lovely if you like textural contrast. Sherry wine, Pedro Ximenez to be exact, is the pairing of choice.

SERVES 8–10

ALMOND COOKIE CRUST

- 140 g shortbread biscuits (Bakers Eet-Sum-Mor)
- 50 g almonds, roasted
- 2.5 ml ground mixed spice
- 10 ml honey
- 50 g butter, melted

CHEESECAKE FILLING

- 500 g cream cheese, room temperature
- 3 whole eggs
- 2 egg yolks
- 150 g castor sugar
- 250 ml fresh cream
- 30 ml cake wheat flour
- 5 ml vanilla paste
- a pinch of salt

Preheat the oven to 200°C. Line the base and sides of an 18 cm springform cake tin with baking paper. To prevent leakage, use two sheets of paper. The collar should extend 2–3 cm above the rim.

FOR THE COOKIE CRUST, process the biscuits, nuts and spice until fine crumb texture. Add the honey and butter, and pulse to combine. Tip the mixture into the tin and press down firmly on the base only. Chill while you make the filling.

FOR THE FILLING, place all the cheesecake filling ingredients in a blender and blitz until smooth. Set aside to rest for 5 minutes. Pour the filling into the cake tin and tap lightly on the counter to remove visible air bubbles. Bake for 50 minutes, then turn the oven temperature up to 230°C and bake for a further 10–15 minutes.

Cool to room temperature. Cover the top with foil, then chill overnight in the tin. Loosen the mould gently before peeling off the paper collar.

COOK'S NOTE: The flour component is negligible; even so it helps enormously towards a set texture.

SICILIAN ORANGE TORTE

Baking with butter substitutes, olive oil in particular, not only supports the longevity of a bake (moistness), but adds dimensional intensity to the crumb. You'll pick up on a beautiful grassy depth mingled with wintry citrus oils.

We adore this cake as is, or with softly whipped cream and lemon curd.

SERVES 12

70 g golden sultanas
30 ml Cointreau or orange juice
1 large whole orange, skin on
zest of 2 oranges
3 eggs
210 g castor sugar
125 ml extra virgin olive oil
125 ml buttermilk or sour cream
5 ml vanilla extract
175 g self-raising flour
80 g almond flour
2.5 ml baking powder
1.25 ml fine salt
50 g pine nuts or almond flakes
15 ml icing sugar, to finish

Preheat the oven to 180°C. Line and butter a 23 cm round, loose-bottomed baking tin with baking paper.

Combine the sultanas and Cointreau or orange juice in a small bowl. Set aside to macerate and plump up (heating in the microwave for 15 seconds will aid the process) while you mix the batter.

Cut the orange in half and remove the seeds and white centre pith. Slice the orange into chunks. Add to a blender along with the zest, eggs, castor sugar, olive oil, buttermilk or sour cream, and vanilla. Blend until smooth.

Sift the self-raising flour, almond flour, baking powder and salt into a mixing bowl. Add the orange purée and whisk until just combined. Fold in the sultanas along with any resting juices.

Scrape the batter into the prepared tin and smooth over with the back of a spoon. Scatter the pine nuts or almond flakes on top. Bake for 50–55 minutes.

Rest in the tin for 10 minutes. Run a knife around the sides to loosen before unmoulding. Transfer to a wire rack to cool completely. Dust lightly with icing sugar to finish.

LEOPARD CHOCOLATE BISCUIT CAKE

For the leopard effect, cut the biscuits into smallish squares. It really is an anything goes kind of recipe. Chopped nuts, dried cherries, apricots, that sort of thing. Unashamedly rich with a fudge-like texture.

SERVES 12–14

125 g butter
120 g dark chocolate (70%), roughly chopped
80 ml honey or golden syrup
25 g cocoa powder
5 ml vanilla extract
a pinch of Maldon sea salt flakes
250 g Bakers Eet-Sum-Mor biscuits, roughly chopped
100 g dried cranberries

TOPPING
150 g milk chocolate, roughly chopped
30 ml full-cream milk
15 ml olive oil
15 ml boiling water

melted chocolate, to drizzle (optional)
cocoa nibs, to finish (optional)

Line and butter a 15 cm loose-bottomed cake tin.

Place the butter, dark chocolate, honey or syrup, and cocoa in a heatproof bowl set over a pan of gently simmering water. Stir gently until melted, then remove from the heat. Add the vanilla and salt, and whisk with a balloon whisk to break up any dry cocoa clumps.

Fold in the biscuits and cranberries. Scrape into the cake tin and press the mixture down firmly. Chill for several hours until set.

FOR THE TOPPING, melt the milk chocolate and milk gently. Whisk in the olive oil and water. Spread the topping over the set cake and chill for 2 hours.

Unmould carefully and place on a cake plate. Drizzle with a little extra melted chocolate and scatter with cocoa nibs, if you like.

SHORTBREAD MATCHSTICKS WITH LIME ZEST

Only once I'd styled the shortbread did I realize they looked exactly like Lion matches, hence the name. However you choose to shape them, they're crumbly, wonderfully crisp and just what tea needs. Orange zest, instead of lime zest, works well too, especially with dark chocolate.

MAKES 32

- 180 g butter, room temperature
- 90 g castor sugar
- zest of 2 limes
- 5 ml vanilla extract
- 250 g cake wheat flour
- 60 g cornflour
- 1.25 ml fine salt
- 120 g dark or white chocolate, melted (optional)

Line a 22 cm square tin with baking paper. Extend the paper over the rim to create lifting handles.

Cream the butter, castor sugar, lime zest and vanilla together.

Sift in the flour, cornflour and salt. Whisk on a low speed until combined. Tip the dough into the tin and press down firmly. Smooth over the top. Chill for 45–60 minutes.

Preheat the oven to 160°C.

Carefully lift the shortbread out of the tin using the paper handles. Using a bench scrape or smooth knife, cut down the centre, dividing the dough into two equal halves. Cut into matchsticks, about 12 mm in width. Arrange on a baking sheet and bake for 30–32 minutes until lightly golden.

Rest on the tray for 10 minutes, then transfer to a wire rack to cool completely.

Dip the tips in melted chocolate. Once set, store in an airtight container.

WHISKY & OLIVE OIL CHOCOLATE TRUFFLES

Strikingly compatible, with fruity notes surfacing from both the chocolate and olive oil. Intentionally rich and dark. To lessen the intensity, use equal quantities of milk and dark chocolate for the truffle mixture.

MAKES 20

150 g dark chocolate (70%), roughly chopped
100 ml coconut milk
30 ml honey
22.5 ml whisky
15 ml extra virgin olive oil
2.5 ml Maldon sea salt flakes

COATING OPTIONS
cocoa, sifted, for dusting
cocoa nibs
120 g milk chocolate, melted, for dipping

Place the chocolate, coconut milk, honey and whisky in a heatproof bowl set over a pan of simmering water. Heat gently for several minutes. Carefully lift the bowl from the saucepan and whisk until glossy and smooth.

Cool for several minutes before stirring in the olive oil and salt. Once the chocolate is at room temperature, cover and chill until set, several hours or overnight.

Roll into balls. Coat the truffles in cocoa or cocoa nibs. Alternatively, dip in milk chocolate.

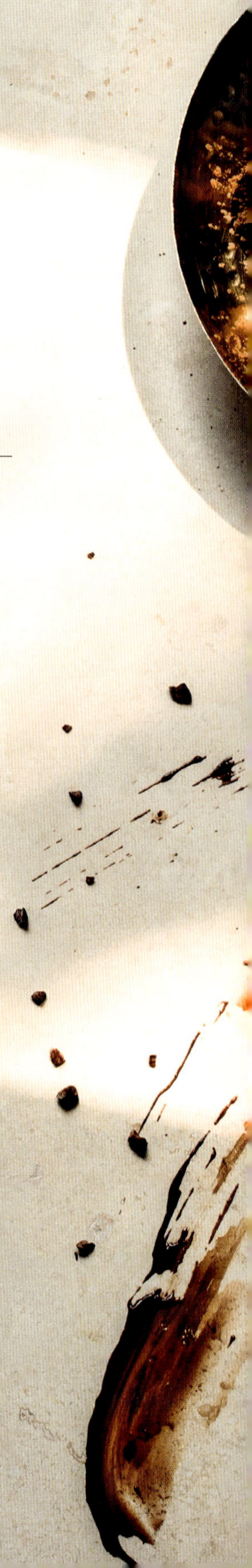

SPICED PLUM 'MEMBRILLO'

With a similar texture to quince cheese or membrillo, although not quite as granular. Recently, I started adding a pinch of Sichuan pepper, not too much though. Pair with a creamy blue or camembert. (A spoonful stirred into meaty casseroles and stews adds a fruity sweetness to the gravy.)

MAKES 400 ML

1 kg ripe red-fleshed plums, halved and pitted
500 ml water
2 slivers lemon peel
4 whole cloves
2 star anise
450 g granulated white sugar
30 ml lemon juice
15 ml balsamic vinegar

Roughly chop the plums into bite-size pieces. Place in a deep saucepan along with the water. Bring up to the boil, cover with a lid and simmer for 35–40 minutes. The fruit needs to be completely collapsed, almost mushy. When cool enough to handle, pour the softened fruit and liquid into a strainer. Using a wooden spoon or balloon whisk – I find the latter to work best – expel as much of the pulp as possible.

Measure the pulp volume. It should be close to 750 ml. Add the fruit pulp to the saucepan, along with the lemon peel, cloves, star anise, sugar and lemon juice. Heat gently, stirring all the while, until the sugar is dissolved. Turn the heat up and boil rapidly for 35–40 minutes. Stir in the balsamic vinegar.

Strain to remove the solids, then pour into hot, sterilized jars and seal. Store in the fridge for up to 2 months.

COOK'S NOTE: Lovely paired with Seed & Nut Oat Bread (page 62).

GATHERED FEASTS

–INDIAN | MOROCCAN | ITALIAN–

Escapism through food extends beyond well-trodden terrains, to unfamiliar places, appeasing our curiosity and satiating an adventurous palate. If your heart quickens at the thought of gathering friends and family around the table, then come with me. Our vicarious adventure will transport us to the intoxicating food markets of Marrakesh, to the colourful streets of India, before stopping off in Italy for a convivial celebration of good food and wine. Eating together is as much about culture and tradition as it is about a sense of place. And, although the world around us continues to change, this age-old practice remains one of life's simplest, most memorable pleasures.

When I think of feasts, words like ample, abundance, joyful come to mind. Occasions call for a more considered approach than everyday food. The suggested menus are by no means prescriptive, more a nudge towards intertwining flavours that flow seamlessly together. Whether cooking for an intimate party of two or an extended table of many, it's in the spirit of communion that even the simplest food becomes a feast, one that will be remembered long after the dishes are stacked away and the lights dimmed.

INDIAN

CHOLE PALAK

A North Indian curry, made with spinach (*palak*) and chickpeas (*chole*). Here, it serves as an opener; although, if you're making it for a midweek supper and want more than just chickpeas, halved cherry tomatoes or sweet potato chunks are good additions.

SERVES 4

coconut or vegetable oil, for cooking
1 brown onion, diced
1–2 cloves garlic, minced
15 ml freshly grated ginger
5 ml cumin seeds
10 ml ground coriander
5 ml garam masala
2.5 ml ground turmeric
1.25 ml chilli powder
200 g (1 small bunch) spinach or Swiss chard, shredded
1 x 400 g tin chopped tomatoes
5 ml granulated white sugar
125 ml vegetable or chicken stock
fine salt and freshly ground black pepper
1 x 400 g tin chickpeas, rinsed and drained
5 ml lemon juice
125 ml double-cream yoghurt, to serve

Heat 15 ml oil in a large saucepan. Add the onion and sauté over a medium heat until softened, about 10 minutes. Stir in the garlic and ginger, and cook for another minute.

Add the cumin seeds and toast for about a minute before adding all the remaining spices, including the chilli powder. Stir to coat the onions in the spice mix. Place the spinach on top, and cook until slightly softened and wilted.

Add the tomatoes, sugar and stock. Season lightly with salt and black pepper, cover partially and simmer for about 15 minutes.

Stir in the chickpeas and cook for 10 minutes or until the sauce is thickened and reduced. Add the lemon juice. Taste and adjust seasoning, if needed.

Swirl the yoghurt on top just before serving.

CHICKEN MADRAS CURRY WITH PAPRIKA ROAST POTATOES

A madras curry is fairly hot, with a distinctive orangey-red sauce. Ground poppy seeds add a slightly spicy, nutty taste and are often used in Indian cooking to help thicken sauces. White poppy seeds are traditional, although the blue-black variety are more readily available. Macadamia nuts do a wonderful job of furthering the nutty undertones, so we'll add these too.

SERVES 6

coconut or vegetable oil, for cooking
1 large red onion, finely diced
1 clove garlic, minced
15 ml freshly grated ginger
900 g chicken thighs, skinless and deboned, halved
fine salt and freshly ground black pepper
30 ml tomato paste
1 x 400 g tin chopped tomatoes
1 x 400 g tin coconut milk
1 cinnamon stick
3 bay leaves
15 ml lemon juice

MADRAS SPICE MIX
15 ml coriander seeds
5 ml fennel seeds
3 whole cloves
15 ml poppy seeds
35 g macadamia nuts, roughly chopped
5 cardamom pods, crushed, husks removed, and lightly ground
2.5 ml ground turmeric
5 ml paprika
5 ml Kashmiri chilli powder
2.5 ml dried red chilli flakes

PAPRIKA ROAST POTATOES
500 g baby potatoes, rinsed and boiled until fork tender
30 ml olive oil
5 ml smoked paprika
fine salt and freshly ground black pepper
fresh coriander, to finish (optional)

FIRST MAKE THE MADRAS SPICE MIX. Dry-toast the coriander, fennel, cloves, poppy seeds and macadamia nuts in a pan until fragrant. Set aside to cool. Transfer to a spice grinder and pulse until finely ground. Combine the ground spices with the cardamom, turmeric, paprika, Kashmiri chilli and chilli flakes.

FOR THE CURRY, heat 15 ml oil in a deep saucepan. Add the onion and sauté until softened and caramelized, about 15 minutes. Stir in the garlic and ginger, and cook for another minute. Add the Madras Spice Mix and toast for several minutes until deeply fragrant.

Drizzle in another 15 ml oil, then add the chicken. Stir to coat the chicken in the spices and sear on all sides. Season lightly with salt and black pepper. Add a splash of water, about 45 ml, to deglaze and lift off all the sticky bits on the base of the pan. Stir in the tomato paste, chopped tomatoes, coconut milk, cinnamon, bay leaves and lemon juice. Cover and simmer for about 40 minutes.

FOR THE ROAST POTATOES, preheat the oven to 200°C. Arrange the potatoes in a roasting tin. Press down lightly to burst the skins. Drizzle with olive oil and season with paprika, salt and pepper. Roast for 1 hour, turning them over halfway through the cooking time.

Add the potatoes to the curry just before serving. Sprinkle with fresh coriander and serve with the Pear & Sultana Chutney (opposite).

COOK'S NOTE: Most curries taste better the following day, in which case roast the potatoes an hour or so before serving.

PEAR & SULTANA CHUTNEY

Sautéing the shallots and toasting the aromatics, rather than throwing everything in together at once, concentrates the sweetness of the shallots and blooms the spices. Besides being the best curry companion, fruit chutneys add heaps of tangy personality to cheese boards, so maybe double the recipe and store it in the fridge for your next drinks party.

MAKES 250 ML

vegetable oil, for cooking
1 shallot or small brown onion, finely diced
1 clove garlic, finely minced
15 ml freshly grated ginger
5 ml cumin seeds
2.5 ml mustard seeds
1.25 ml ground cinnamon
1.25 ml ground mixed spice
a pinch of dried red chilli flakes
2 large pears, peeled, cored and cut into cubes
45 g sultanas
70 g brown sugar
60 ml apple cider vinegar
10 ml lemon juice
fine salt and freshly ground black pepper, to taste

Heat 15 ml oil in a saucepan. Add the shallot or onion, and sauté until softened, about 8 minutes. Stir in the garlic and ginger, and cook for another minute or so.

Add all the spices, including the chilli flakes, and stir to coat the onions. Once fragrant, add the pears, sultanas, sugar, vinegar and lemon juice. Season with salt and a few twists of black pepper. Cover and simmer over a medium heat for 25–30 minutes. The liquid should be completely reduced, and the chutney sticky and glossy. Transfer to a sterilized jar and seal.

COOK'S NOTE: *Keeps well for 6–8 weeks, chilled. If the pears are smallish, use three.*

ORANGE SALAD WITH PICKLED ONION & CREAMY TAHINI SAUCE

More of a palate cleanser than a full-scale salad, but sensationally colourful and refreshing. Tahini, while not remotely Indian, adds a creaminess to the sauce. Blood oranges are gorgeously showy, with hints of raspberries, cherry and grapefruit. If you spot these beauties at the market, snap them up. Here, I've opted for Cara Cara oranges.

SERVES 6

3–4 Cara Cara oranges, peeled and thinly sliced
60 ml pomegranate seeds
purple micro herbs, to finish
2 spring onions, thinly sliced
30 g pistachio slivers, toasted
extra virgin olive oil, for drizzling
Maldon sea salt flakes and freshly ground black pepper, to finish

QUICK RED ONION PICKLE
45 ml red wine vinegar
10 ml castor sugar
2.5 ml salt
½ red onion, peeled and thinly sliced

CREAMY TAHINI SAUCE
60 ml Greek yoghurt
15 ml tahini
zest of 1 lemon, plus 15 ml juice
10 ml apple cider vinegar
60 ml water
fine salt and freshly ground black pepper, to taste

START BY MAKING THE ONION PICKLE. Combine the vinegar, sugar and salt in a small bowl. Warm slightly, stirring to dissolve the sugar. Add the onion, then set aside for 15 minutes.

FOR THE TAHINI SAUCE, place all the ingredients in a small bowl and whisk to combine.

Arrange the orange slices on a large serving plate. Drizzle over half the creamy tahini sauce. Serve the remaining sauce alongside.

Drain the onion pickle and lay over the oranges. Scatter with pomegranate seeds, herbs, spring onions and pistachios. Finish with a drizzle of your best extra virgin olive oil, a pinch of flaky sea salt and black pepper.

COOK'S NOTE: Prepare all the components ahead of time. Assemble just before serving.

PISTACHIO & CARDAMOM PEAR CAKE

At first, you'll wonder if there's something wrong with the recipe, because it's just plain weird. However, it will turn out to be the best thing you've baked in forever. Delicately perfumed, with a sort of cheesecake crust and a frangipane-pudding centre. If you're after an intriguing and less sweet dessert, this is the one to make.

SERVES 10–12

- 260 g cake wheat flour
- 50 g almond flour
- 1.25 ml fine salt
- 5 ml ground cinnamon
- 7 cardamom pods, crushed, husks removed, and finely ground
- 225 g soft brown sugar
- 200 g butter, melted
- 2 eggs, lightly whisked
- 250 ml sour cream
- 5 ml vanilla extract
- 5 ml bicarbonate of soda
- 2 pears, ripe but firm, cored and thinly sliced
- 30 g pistachio nuts, halved
- honey, for brushing
- icing sugar, to finish

CINNAMON HONEY CREAM

- 250 ml fresh cream
- 30 ml honey
- 2.5 ml ground cinnamon

Preheat the oven to 180°C. Line and butter a 23 cm springform cake tin with baking paper.

Sift together the cake wheat flour, almond flour, salt, cinnamon and cardamom. Add the sugar and mix. I use a balloon whisk here to ensure the sugar is evenly distributed. Drizzle in the warm melted butter and mix to combine. The mixture will have a sandy texture.

Weigh the crumb mixture, then scrape half into the prepared tin. Press into the base of the tin and smooth over with the back of a spoon.

To the remaining crumb mixture, add the eggs and whisk with a handheld mixer. Add the sour cream, vanilla and bicarbonate of soda, and whisk until smooth. Spread the batter over the base. Arrange the sliced pears on top. Scatter the nuts in between the pears. Bake for 45–50 minutes, or until the top springs back. Brush the pears with warm honey while the cake is still hot.

Cool in the tin before unmoulding and dusting lightly with icing sugar.

FOR THE CREAM, whisk the fresh cream, honey and cinnamon together until softly peaked. Dust lightly with extra cinnamon before serving with the cake.

MOROCCAN

LENTIL HUMMUS WITH CRISPY SPROUT CRUMBLE

The recipe for both hummus and crumble makes more than you'll need, unless, of course, it's an expansive feast or your guests are hummus mad. Save it for a midweek lunch. I love it on sourdough toast for breakfast – with an egg or sliced avocado.

MAKES 500 ML

LENTIL HUMMUS

- 90 g red lentils
- 1 x 400 g tin cannellini beans, rinsed and drained
- 2 cloves garlic, roasted
- 80 ml tahini
- 5 ml cumin seeds, toasted and ground
- 5 ml coriander seeds, toasted and ground
- 1.25 ml dried red chilli flakes
- 2.5 ml smoked paprika
- 30 ml lemon juice
- 30 ml olive oil
- fine salt and freshly ground black pepper, to taste
- 30–45 ml cold water

CRISPY SPROUT CRUMBLE

- 30 ml white and black sesame seeds
- 30 ml sunflower seeds
- olive oil, for frying
- 60 g mixed sprouts
- zest of ½ lemon, plus 5 ml juice
- fine salt and freshly ground black pepper, to taste
- several sprigs of fresh mint, leaves picked and roughly chopped
- extra virgin olive oil, for drizzling

FOR THE HUMMUS, rinse the lentils several times to remove any grit, then drain. Add the lentils to a saucepan with 250 ml water and a generous pinch of salt. Bring up to the boil. Simmer for 15–18 minutes, until completely softened. The lentils will look a little mushy, with most of the water evaporated. Set aside to cool.

Scrape the lentils into a processor, then add the beans and garlic. Process until smooth. Add all the remaining ingredients and blitz once more. Drizzle in the water and process until smooth.

TO MAKE THE CRUMBLE, dry-toast the sesame seeds in a pan for several minutes. Tip onto a plate. Add the sunflower seeds to the pan and toast until golden, 3–4 minutes, then add to the sesame seeds.

Heat 10 ml olive oil in the same pan. Add the sprouts and cook for several minutes. Stir through the lemon zest and juice. Season lightly with salt and black pepper. Remove from the heat, then add to the seeds along with the mint.

Spread the hummus onto a serving plate and top with the sprout crumble. Drizzle generously with olive oil. Serve with warm flatbread.

BROWN RICE PILAF WITH CARAMELIZED ONIONS & PICKLED CURRANTS

There's no need for a turned-out dome, but it's the work of seconds and looks rather fabulous. Be patient with the onions. They need more than softening. Bronzed and sweet is what we're looking for, as if they were heading towards a French onion soup.

SERVES 4–6

- olive oil, for cooking, plus extra for drizzling
- 2 large brown onions, sliced into half moons
- fine salt and freshly ground black pepper
- zest of ½ lemon
- 5 ml cumin seeds
- 200 g brown basmati rice, cooked as per manufacturer's instructions (yields 625 ml once cooked)
- 10 ml lemon juice
- 40 g flaked almonds, toasted
- a generous handful each of fresh coriander and flat-leaf parsley

PICKLED CURRANTS

- 45 ml red wine vinegar
- 10 ml castor sugar
- 2.5 ml fine salt
- 40 g currants

START BY MAKING THE PICKLE. Combine the vinegar, sugar and salt in a small bowl. Warm slightly, then add the currants. Set aside to macerate, 20–25 minutes.

Heat 30 ml oil in a pan. Add the onions and a pinch of salt. Cook over a medium heat for 20–25 minutes until completely caramelized. Reserve 15 ml of the onions for finishing.

Add the lemon zest and cumin to the onions and cook until fragrant, about 2 minutes. Tip in the cooked rice and stir to coat. Add the lemon juice and season lightly with salt and a couple of twists of black pepper. Drizzle with a little olive oil to moisten the rice.

Drain the currants and set aside a spoonful for finishing. Add the remaining currants, almonds, herbs and 15 ml olive to the rice and fold through.

Transfer the rice to a lightly oiled 1.2 litre pudding bowl. Press down firmly to compact. I use a small cake board to cover the rice, with a heavy tin placed on top. Set aside for 5 minutes before inverting onto a rimmed plate. (If necessary, place in a warm oven to keep warm, or microwave for several minutes to reheat.)

Finish with the reserved onions and the pickled currants.

SOUR CREAM CUCUMBER SALAD WITH NIGELLA SEEDS

Essential for balancing spicy heat. Almost a raita, though slightly more delicate. The sour cream isn't offensive or prominent, as one would think, but just there, with an edgy tang. Salting the cucumber removes excess water and helps keep the dressing creamy. Tempting as it is, don't skip this step.

SERVES 4

1 English cucumber, thinly sliced
2.5 ml fine salt

SOUR CREAM DRESSING
10 ml apple cider vinegar
5 ml lemon juice
5 ml granulated white sugar
freshly ground black pepper
60 ml sour cream
60 ml Greek yoghurt
several sprigs of fresh dill, leaves picked
5 ml nigella seeds
extra virgin olive oil, for drizzling

Place the cucumber in a bowl and scatter over the salt. Toss to coat, then transfer to a colander. Set aside for about 20 minutes to allow the water to drain. Rinse well under cold water, making sure most of the salt is removed. Drain well, then pat dry with paper towel.

FOR THE DRESSING, whisk together the vinegar, lemon juice, sugar and black pepper in a mixing bowl. Add the sour cream and yoghurt, and whisk to combine.

Add the cucumber and toss lightly to coat. Transfer to a serving plate and finish with dill sprigs, nigella seeds and a drizzle of olive oil.

CHICKEN TAGINE WITH ALMOND & PRESERVED LEMON SALSA

A ceremoniously opulent dish, prepared for special occasions. Scented with saffron and a heady melange of fragrant spices, it is indeed feast-worthy. For those who prefer red meat, replace the chicken with beef shin pieces or lamb cubes, in which case, cook in the oven for about 3 hours at 180°C, adding a little more water, if needed.

SERVES 6

- 1.2 kg (10 pieces) chicken pieces, bone-in and skinless (thighs and drumsticks)
- fine salt and freshly ground black pepper
- olive oil, for cooking
- 2 brown onions, finely diced
- 2 cloves garlic, minced
- 15 ml freshly grated ginger
- 10 ml smoked paprika
- 5 ml cumin seeds
- 7.5 ml ground cumin
- 3.75 ml ground coriander
- 5 ml ground turmeric
- 2.5 ml dried red chilli flakes
- 30 ml tomato paste
- 1 x 400 g tin chopped tomatoes
- 500 ml chicken stock
- a pinch of saffron threads
- 1 cinnamon stick
- 15 ml honey
- 30 ml butter
- 120 g (about 12) Turkish apricots
- 10 ml lemon juice
- fresh coriander, to finish

Season the chicken on both sides with salt and black pepper.

Heat 15 ml oil in a deep cast-iron saucepan. Brown the chicken on both sides, working in batches. Remove and set aside.

Add a little more oil to the pan along with the onions and sauté until softened. Add the garlic and ginger, and cook for another minute. Stir in all the aromatics, up to and including the chilli flakes, mixing to coat the onions. Add the tomato paste, chopped tomatoes, stock, saffron, cinnamon stick and honey. Bring the sauce up to the boil, then return the chicken to the pan, submerging the pieces in the sauce.

Cover with a lid and simmer for 45–50 minutes until the sauce is reduced and the chicken cooked through. Stir in the butter, apricots and lemon juice. Finish with fresh coriander. Serve the salsa alongside.

ALMOND & PRESERVED LEMON SALSA Combine 50 g toasted and roughly chopped almonds, 45 ml lemon juice, 15 ml finely chopped preserved lemon, a handful of chopped fresh mint, 15 ml honey and 60 ml olive oil. Season with salt and black pepper.

PISTACHIO & WALNUT BAKLAVA

Said to have been brought to the Ottoman empire by the Turks in the 15th century, this phyllo-drenched pastry has captivated and charmed sweet tooth lovers the world over. Rather than cloyingly sweet, this version is more nut-focused than it is sugary. When the former courses have been resplendent, a small mouthful of sweet makes for the perfect closure, along with a strong black coffee.

MAKES A 28 CM ROUND

250 g pistachios
100 g walnuts
5 ml ground cinnamon
4 cardamom pods, crushed, husks removed, and finely ground
45 ml castor sugar
500 g phyllo pastry (17 sheets), cut into rounds to fit the baking tin
120 g butter, melted

SYRUP
300 ml water
160 g granulated white sugar
80 ml honey
15 ml lemon juice
zest of 1 orange
2 lemon slices
2 cinnamon sticks
a pinch of fine salt
5 ml rosewater

START BY MAKING THE SYRUP. Place all the ingredients, except the rosewater, in a small saucepan. Simmer over a low heat for 7–8 minutes. Stir in the rosewater, then set aside to cool completely.

Preheat the oven to 170°C. Butter a 28 cm round baking tin.

Place the pistachios, walnuts, cinnamon, cardamom and sugar in a processor, and blitz in short spurts until the nuts are coarsely chopped, but still with some texture.

Brush seven sheets of pastry with melted butter, stacking one on top of the other whilst layering in the baking tin. Scatter half the nut mixture on top. Layer five more buttered sheets of phyllo on top of the nut mixture, pressing gently to compress. Cover with the remaining nuts, using your fingertips to spread them evenly. Brush the remaining five sheets of phyllo with butter and place on top. The final phyllo sheet should be well buttered to ensure a deeply golden colour.

With a sharp knife, cut the pastry halfway through in the desired pattern, being careful not to cut all the way through. Bake for 55–60 minutes. Cover with foil halfway through the baking time if the top darkens too much.

Pour the cooled syrup over the hot pastry as soon as it comes out of the oven. Set aside for several hours before cutting through.

ITALIAN

LEMONY CACIO E PEPE RISOTTO

The secret to a good risotto – besides good ingredients – is stirring. It's really that simple. Risotto is needy, requiring a fully focused cook and 30 minutes. Bear in mind that the first course – Primo – is considered a starter, so portion sizes should lean more towards conservative than ample.

SERVES 6

30 ml olive oil
30 ml butter, divided
1 shallot, finely diced
2.5 ml coarsely ground black pepper
zest of 1 lemon
2 sprigs of fresh thyme, leaves picked
200 g arborio rice
100 ml white wine (chenin blanc)
1 litre hot chicken stock
55 g parmesan, finely grated
15 ml lemon juice
grated pecorino, to serve
fine salt, to taste
extra virgin olive oil, to serve

Heat 30 ml olive oil and 15 ml butter in a deep saucepan. Add the shallot and cook over a low heat until softened but still pale, 5–7 minutes. Stir in the pepper and lemon zest, and sizzle until the oil smells fragrant, just a minute or so.

Add the thyme and rice. Cook for 2 minutes, stirring constantly. Once the rice smells nutty and sounds almost 'glassy' against the pan, deglaze with the wine and reduce by half.

Keep the stock warm by placing it in a saucepan over a medium heat.

Ladle in the stock gradually, stirring all the while. The stock should be fully absorbed before adding the next ladle. Cooking times will vary between 22–25 minutes. Check that the rice is al dente and the consistency creamy.

Remove from the heat and rest for 2 minutes with the lid on. Stir in the parmesan, lemon juice and the remaining butter. Season to taste. At this point, you may want to loosen the risotto by adding a little hot water.

Divide the risotto between six shallow bowls. Serve with grated pecorino and a drizzle of extra virgin olive oil.

TRIVIA: Cacio e pepe, Rome's famed pasta dish, epitomizes simple cooking – spaghetti, pecorino Romano and black pepper.

BROCCOLINI & GREEN BEANS WITH PESTO DRESSING

Blanching vegetables might seem like drudgery, but it helps retain the bright green colour we're after. They need to be crisp, barely cooked. You can prepare the veggies ahead of time, the day before even, then assemble while the fillet (page 231) is in the oven. Serve warm or at room temperature, with plenty of parmesan.

SERVES 6

250 g broccolini, trimmed
350 g green beans
olive oil, for cooking
fine salt and freshly ground black pepper
1 x 400 g tin cannellini beans, rinsed and drained
1 lemon, thinly sliced and seared in a pan for 2 minutes per side
50 g parmesan shavings
fresh basil, to finish
extra virgin olive oil, for drizzling

PESTO DRESSING
45 ml olive oil
30 ml lemon juice
60 ml basil pesto
zest of 1 lemon
fine salt and freshly ground black pepper

FIRST MAKE THE PESTO DRESSING by whisking together all the ingredients in a small bowl.

Blanche the broccoli in salted water for about 3 minutes. Place in ice water immediately, then drain. Do the same for the green beans.

Heat 15 ml olive oil in a wide-based pan until hot. Add the broccoli and sear on a fierce heat for 2 minutes. Season lightly, then add a heaped tablespoon of the pesto dressing, tossing to coat. Transfer to a plate. Repeat the process with the green beans.

Season the cannellini beans lightly with salt and black pepper. Add 15 ml of the dressing to the cannellini beans and toss to coat. Transfer to a serving plate. Arrange the broccoli and green beans on top, along with the lemon slices. Drizzle over the remaining dressing.

Finish with parmesan shavings, fresh basil and a drizzle of extra virgin olive oil.

FILLET OF BEEF WITH CHARRED SPRING ONION & PINE NUT SALSA VERDE

With its buttery soft texture, beef fillet is considered *the* premium cut. When cooking, aim for rare or medium-rare to retain its tender juiciness.

Charring the spring onions is optional, but adds an edgy smokiness that complements the beef beautifully. The crushed ice, added to the salsa, helps keep the colour vibrant and fresh.

SERVES 6–8

10 ml paprika
15 ml dried thyme
5 ml dried oregano
2 sprigs of fresh rosemary, leaves picked and finely chopped, plus several whole sprigs for roasting
7.5 ml Maldon sea salt flakes
freshly ground black pepper
1.2 kg centre-cut fillet of beef
olive oil, for cooking

CHARRED SPRING ONION & PINE NUT SALSA VERDE
olive oil, for cooking
3 spring onions, thickly sliced
25 g each of loosely packed flat-leaf parsley and basil leaves
1–2 cloves garlic
2–3 anchovy fillets
30 ml capers
80 ml extra virgin olive oil
15 ml red wine vinegar
15 ml lemon juice
3.75 ml Maldon sea salt flakes
freshly ground black pepper
30 g pine nuts, toasted
1 small ice cube, crushed (no more than 10 ml)

In a small bowl, combine the paprika, thyme, oregano, rosemary, salt and black pepper.

Pat the fillet dry with paper towel. Tie with butcher's string, spacing 2 cm between each knot. Rub the herb and spice mix over the beef, cover and set aside for 30 minutes, or overnight in the fridge, if time allows.

Preheat the oven to 200°C.

Heat a wide-based ovenproof pan until smoking hot. Drizzle the fillet generously with olive oil. Place in the pan and sear until caramelized, without turning, for about 2 minutes until the meat forms a deeply golden crust. Turn and repeat on the remaining three sides.

Tuck the extra rosemary sprigs under the fillet. Transfer the pan to the oven and roast, uncovered, for 20–23 minutes or until done to your liking. Cover the fillet with foil and rest for at least 8 minutes before carving.

MEANWHILE, MAKE THE SALSA. Heat 10 ml olive oil in a pan. Add the spring onions and scorch over a high heat, just a minute or two per side. Set aside to cool.

Place all the remaining salsa ingredients, except the spring onions, pine nuts and ice, in a processor and blitz to a roughly textured sauce. Add the ice and blitz briefly to combine. Spoon into a bowl and stir in the spring onions and pine nuts. Serve alongside the fillet.

COOK'S NOTES: Deep caramelization brings out the natural sugars and forms a flavourful crust. This is best done in a pan, with direct heat, then finished in the oven. Alternatively, cook over the coals for an unmistakable smokiness.

Always bring the meat to room temperature before cooking.

RED WINE & CARDAMOM FIG ICE CREAM

If you're in two minds as to whether you really need an ice cream maker, perhaps this will be the deciding factor. Old school ice cream, the kind you find in a Florentine gelateria, has a buttery smooth texture and otherworldly creaminess. To tone down the richness, I've added milk to the custard, which makes it lighter, more summery.

For the compote, swap the figs for plums or other seasonal fruit, if figs are not quite your cup of tea.

MAKES 1.2 LITRES

VANILLA ICE CREAM
500 ml fresh cream
300 ml full-cream milk
110 g castor sugar, divided
6 egg yolks
7.5 ml vanilla paste
a pinch of fine salt

RED WINE & CARDAMOM FIG COMPOTE
MAKES 400 ML

500 g fresh, ripe black figs, rinsed, stalks removed, and thinly sliced
200 g demerara sugar
250 ml red wine (merlot or shiraz)
60–75 ml lemon juice
zest of 1 lemon
2 cinnamon sticks
8 cardamom pods, crushed, husks removed, and finely ground

FIRST MAKE THE FIG COMPOTE. Place all the ingredients in a deep saucepan. Bring slowly up to the boil, stirring gently, until the sugar is dissolved. Cover partially with a lid and simmer over a medium-high heat for 20–25 minutes.

Remove the lid, increase the heat and allow to bubble away until the figs are broken down and just shy of being jam. Transfer into a clean glass jar and close with a tight-fitting lid.

FOR THE ICE CREAM, heat the cream, milk and half the castor sugar (55 g) in a deep saucepan.

Bring slowly up to the boil, stirring slowly to dissolve the sugar. When tiny bubbles form on the surface, remove from the heat.

Whisk together the egg yolks and remaining castor sugar until light and creamy. Slowly add the hot cream to the egg mixture, whisking continuously.

Return the custard to the pan. Bring slowly up to a simmer over a medium heat. Once the custard starts to thicken or coats the back of the spoon, remove from the heat immediately. Whisk in the vanilla paste and salt.

Transfer the custard to a heatproof bowl. Lay a sheet of cling film directly onto the surface to prevent a skin forming. Once at room temperature, chill in the fridge for several hours, preferably overnight.

Churn the custard in an ice cream maker. Spoon half the ice cream into a 22 x 10 cm loaf tin. Dollop about 100 ml of the fig compote over the ice cream and swirl through. Cover with the rest of the ice cream, followed by another 100 ml of the compote and swirl through. Cover and freeze until firm.

COOK'S NOTES: If you don't have an ice cream maker, use the three-step beating method. Transfer the custard to a freezer-safe bowl and freeze for 1½ hours. Beat with electric beaters to break down the ice crystals. Freeze for 2 hours, then repeat as before. After the third and final beating, swirl through the compote, in layers, cover and freeze until firm.

The compote recipe makes 400 ml – enough for two batches of ice cream or jam for toast.

MEZZE

–SALTY BITS & BOBS–

Mezze, or small sharing plates, hinge around conversational food. They needn't be complicated or vast, but they do need to be interesting and cohesive. It's more about variety than it is quantity. Simple can still be wonderful. Always have good bread on the table, with a bottle of your best olive oil (extra virgin) and perhaps a dip or two. The Quick Butter Bean Mash (page 116), Lentil Hummus (page 214) and Avocado, Pea & Feta Dip (page 247) can all be made ahead, which is helpful if you still have mains to contend with. Others, like the Spinach & Artichoke Dip (page 241) and Pan-grilled Feta (page 238) are best served warm, from oven to table, so factor in a couple of extra minutes here. There's no faffing about when hot cheese is involved.

Cheese boards can be a little more elaborate, a curation of contrasts that complement and arouse delight. I like to include fruit – fresh and preserved – something briny like olives or tapenades, and maybe a jar of pickles with three types of cheese in varying textures and flavours. The cheesemonger's rule suggests something old, something new, something stinky and something blue.

When arranging your board, start with the cheese, or larger elements, then fill in the surrounding spaces with your favourite tasty morsels that will hero the cheese and wow your guests.

PAN-GRILLED FETA WITH CHILLI HONEY BUTTER

The charm of opposites is wildly delicious. Spiced honey butter does an excellent job of reining in the saltiness of fried feta. Anything that involves hot cheese needs to be eaten straightaway, so make sure your guests are ready and waiting to dive in.

SERVES 4

olive oil, for cooking
30 ml cake wheat flour
1 egg, lightly whisked
40 g panko breadcrumbs (or homemade dry breadcrumbs)
30 ml sesame seeds
freshly ground black pepper
100 g block feta, blotted with paper towel
crackers or pita breads, to serve

CHILLI HONEY BUTTER
30 ml butter, melted and warm
45 ml honey
2.5 ml dried red chilli flakes

FOR THE HONEY BUTTER, lightly whisk all the ingredients together in a small bowl until combined.

Prepare the dredging bowls – one with the flour, the second with the whisked egg. Combine the breadcrumbs, sesame seeds and a few turns of black pepper in a third bowl.

Heat 15 ml olive oil in a non-stick pan.

Coat the feta in the flour, then dip into the egg wash. Dredge in the crumbs, turning to coat evenly on all sides.

Place in the hot oil and cook over a medium heat until golden and crisp, about 3 minutes per side. Drain on paper towel.

Place the feta on a serving dish and drizzle with the honey butter. Serve immediately with crackers or pita breads.

BURRATA WITH ROAST TOMATOES & SMOKY CHILLI CRISP

Less of a recipe, and more of a pairing. You'll need fresh burrata, Kitchen Staple Balsamic Roast Tomatoes (page 112) and Smoky Chilli Crisp (page 18). And good bread.

SPINACH & ARTICHOKE DIP

Some things just never go out of style, do they? You could leave the leeks out of this retro dip, but alliums are particularly good with cheese, so include them if you can. I make this ahead of time, then slide it into the oven just before guests arrive. There's a lot of cheese, but also spinach. Shut one eye, you'll be fine.

SERVES 8–10

olive oil, for cooking
2–3 medium leeks, washed and cut into coins
200 g baby spinach, rinsed and drained
fine salt and freshly ground black pepper
250 g cream cheese, at room temperature
125 ml sour cream
45 ml milk
30 ml mayonnaise
50 g parmesan, grated, plus extra for topping
70 g sharp cheddar, grated
100 g mozzarella, grated
150 g artichoke hearts, drained and roughly chopped
2 cloves garlic, minced
a pinch of dried red chilli flakes
zest of ½ lemon
22.5 ml lemon juice
focaccia, to serve

Preheat the oven to 200°C.

Heat 15 ml oil in a wide-based pan. Sauté the leeks over a medium heat until softened and just starting to colour around the edges. Add the spinach, in batches, and wilt down.

Season with salt and black pepper. Set aside to cool slightly.

In a large mixing bowl, whisk together the cream cheese, sour cream, milk and mayonnaise. Add all the remaining ingredients, including the leeks and spinach. Season to taste.

Scrape the mixture into a buttered baking dish and scatter extra parmesan on top.

Bake until golden and bubbling, 25–30 minutes. Cool for 5 minutes. Serve warm with focaccia.

HONEY NUTS WITH ROSEMARY & BLACK PEPPER

When Darren and I started dating, we loved nipping into The Michaelangelo Hotel piano lounge for posh date-night drinks. They served an assortment of nuts in tiny silver-tiered bowls. Thirty years later, we still love a nutty nibble with cocktails.

As the nuts cool, they cluster together, almost like a brittle. Irresistible!

MAKES 300 G

- 15 ml olive oil
- 45 ml maple syrup
- 5 ml paprika
- 1.25 ml dried red chilli flakes
- 1 sprig of fresh rosemary, picked and finely chopped
- 2.5 ml Maldon sea salt flakes
- plenty of freshly ground black pepper
- 300 g raw mixed nuts

Preheat the oven to 180°C. Line a baking sheet with baking paper.

In a mixing bowl, combine all the ingredients, except the nuts. Whisk well to emulsify. Add the nuts and toss to coat.

Spread onto the baking sheet and roast for 15–20 minutes. Cool on the baking sheet. Break into clusters and store in an airtight container.

DUKKAH-DUSTED GOAT'S MILK CHEESE TRUFFLES

As with most truffles, chocolate or otherwise, coatings are customizable. At Christmas time, swap the dukkah for seasonally appropriate finely chopped pistachios and cranberries. Coat the truffles no more than 1 hour before serving.

MAKES 20

250 g cream cheese (medium fat or full fat)
100 g goat's milk cheese
a pinch of Maldon sea salt flakes
freshly ground black pepper
dukkah, for coating

Place the cream cheese in a mixing bowl, and whisk until smooth and creamy.

Add the goat's milk cheese, salt and pepper, and whisk to combine. Cover and chill until firm, about an hour.

Measure out teaspoon amounts and roll into walnut-size balls. Coat in dukkah and arrange on a lined tray. Cover and chill to firm up, about 30 minutes.

WARM HARISSA & HERB DIPPING OIL WITH LEMONY YOGHURT

The oil needs to be warm enough to contrast the coolness of the yoghurt.

SERVES 6

DIPPING OIL
10 ml harissa paste
5 ml sumac
5 ml dried oregano
2.5 ml paprika
5 ml honey or pomegranate molasses
zest of 1 lemon
15 ml lemon juice
60 ml olive oil
several sprigs each of fresh mint and flat-leaf parsley, leaves picked and finely chopped
2.5 ml Maldon sea salt flakes

LEMONY YOGHURT
250 ml Greek yoghurt
zest of 1 lemon
a pinch of Maldon sea salt flakes
focaccia, cut into soldiers, to serve

FOR THE DIPPING OIL, combine the harissa, sumac, oregano, paprika, honey or pomegranate molasses, lemon zest and lemon juice in a heatproof bowl.

Heat the olive oil in a small saucepan until hot, then pour carefully over the harissa mixture. Add the chopped herbs and salt, and whisk to combine.

FOR THE LEMONY YOGHURT, mix together the yoghurt, lemon zest and salt. Spread onto a shallow serving plate. Drizzle half the harissa oil over the yoghurt and swirl through. Serve with the focaccia and the remaining oil alongside, adding more as needed.

COOK'S NOTE: *If you love the meatiness of olives, roughly chop 40 g pitted olives and mix into the dipping oil.*

AVOCADO, PEA & FETA DIP

Creamy yet light, and very good with buttered crostini. I've recommended half a clove of garlic, which seems miserly, but it needs only to support, not overwhelm. Serve as a preamble to an alfresco dinner.

MAKES 300 ML

- 150 g garden peas, plus extra for topping
- 1 avocado
- 60 g creamy feta
- ½ clove garlic
- a handful of fresh mint, leaves picked
- several sprigs of fresh basil, leaves picked
- 22.5 ml fresh lemon juice
- 30 ml extra virgin olive oil, plus extra for drizzling
- fine salt and freshly ground black pepper, to taste
- toasted pumpkin and sunflower seeds, to finish
- sprigs of fresh basil, to finish

If using frozen peas, rinse briefly in warm water to defrost. Drain well.

Place all the ingredients, up to and including the salt and black pepper, in a blender and process until creamy. Taste and adjust the seasoning with an extra squeeze of lemon or pinch of salt to brighten the flavours.

Scatter over the extra peas and toasted seeds. Finish with a generous drizzle of extra virgin olive oil and fresh basil.

PECORINO SHORTBREAD BUTTONS

When it comes to shortbread, savoury or sweet, try as you might, there is nothing that imitates the taste of real butter. The same can be said of well-aged cheese. Use good butter and a cheddar that's been around long enough to develop some personality, at least 6 months, maybe more. These savoury biscuits are on my Christmas bake list year after year, although I wouldn't hold out until then. The crumb is light and crisp. Excellent with prosecco or a summery rosé.

MAKES 36–40

250 g cake wheat flour
2.5 ml fine salt
1.25 ml cayenne pepper
a grinding of black pepper
180 g salted butter, at room temperature
10 ml olive oil
30 g pecorino, grated
70 g strong cheddar, finely grated
35 g mixed seeds (a combination of poppy seeds, and black and white sesame seeds)
1 egg white, lightly whisked

Sift the flour, salt, cayenne pepper and black pepper into a mixing bowl. Add the butter and olive oil to the flour, and mix until the butter is worked in and the dough comes together. Add the pecorino and cheddar cheese and mix to combine.

Divide the dough into two equal pieces. Place each piece on a separate sheet of cling film. Wrap tightly, rolling and twisting the ends until the dough forms a cylinder shape, 20–22 cm long. Chill until firm or freeze until ready to use.

Preheat the oven to 160°C. Line a large baking sheet with baking paper.

Place the seeds on a board and spread out evenly. Brush the surface of each dough roll with egg white and coat in the seeds. Slice into discs, about 7 mm thick. Arrange on the baking sheet and bake for 35–40 minutes until golden. Rest on the baking sheet for 5 minutes before transferring to a wire rack to cool.

COOK'S NOTES: These shortbread buttons taste best when just slightly warm. Heat in a 180°C oven for 2–3 minutes before serving.

Store in an airtight container.

GOLDEN HOUR

–COCKTAILS–

Armed with a handful of basics, it's possible to set up a not-too-shabby drinks cart – gin, vodka, bourbon, prosecco, Angostura bitters, and a simple syrup or two. I've included several infusions, made with ingredients you probably already have in the kitchen, or growing in the garden.

Citrus and botanicals are excellent infusers – grapefruit, tangerine, orange blossom, juniper berries, anything along these lines. Before you chill the glasses and reach for the shaker, it's worth noting that the best cocktails are made with the freshest ingredients and quality spirits. We don't need a cellar-worth, just a few class acts.

WHY SHAKE?

Primarily, it is to mix, but also to chill and dilute. Cocktails containing egg white require vigorous agitation to aerate and froth the white, creating a distinguishable foam top.

AND THE STIRRERS?

If you're an 'old-fashioned' kind of girl, a light swizzle or stir in the same glass, along with the ice, is the sophisticated way to combine flavours.

RUBY GRAPEFRUIT & BASIL COCKTAIL

Gorgeously pink with a creamy flavour and frothy top.

If you're nervous about raw egg whites, aquafaba (chickpea water) is an excellent replacement. Dusting the top with freeze-dried strawberries adds a smidge of fruitiness, a delightful entry point to possibly my favourite cocktail in the book.

SERVES 1

60 ml gin
60 ml freshly squeezed ruby grapefruit juice
30 ml Ruby Grapefruit & Basil Syrup (page 266)
1 egg white or 15 ml aquafaba
ice cubes
freeze-dried strawberries, finely ground (optional)
wafer-thin slice of ruby grapefruit, to finish

Add the gin, grapefruit juice, Grapefruit & Basil Syrup, and egg white or aquafaba to a cocktail shaker. Shake for 15–20 seconds.

Tumble in a few ice cubes and shake vigorously.

Strain into a coupe glass. Sift over the strawberry dust, if using, and finish with a wafer-thin slice of ruby grapefruit. Serve immediately.

COOK'S NOTE: Cocktails are at their best when the glasses are chilled. A couple of minutes in the freezer will do the trick.

ROSÉ & BLACKBERRY SANGRIA

Very often made with apples, but flexible enough to welcome seasonal adaptations, from raspberries to white-fleshed peaches. Serve with cocktail picks to spear the drunken fruit.

SERVES 6

125 ml brandy
60 ml Demerara Simple Syrup (page 266) or agave syrup
1 orange, thinly sliced
1 lemon, thinly sliced
1 x 750 ml bottle rosé wine
125 ml freshly squeezed orange juice
2 nectarines, sliced into slim wedges
200 g blackberries
250 ml sparkling mineral water (optional)
ice, to serve

Add the brandy and syrup to a large pitcher. Stir to combine. Add the orange and lemon slices, and steep for 10 minutes.

Pour in the rosé and orange juice, then add the nectarines and blackberries. Chill for 2 hours.

Just before serving, add the sparkling water, pouring it down the side of the pitcher and stirring gently to combine.

Half fill a tumbler with ice and top up with the sangria. Serve immediately.

ROAST LEMON & BLUEBERRY LEMONADE

Don't bother deseeding the lemons. Once roasted, the pulp is strained. If the lemons are smallish, you'll need at least ten. Try for juicy lemons and in-season, sweet berries.

MAKES 900 ML

8–10 lemons, well rinsed and halved
4 sprigs of fresh thyme
400 g granulated white sugar
280 g blueberries
425 ml water

Preheat the oven to 200°C.

Arrange the lemons, cut side up, in a deep roasting tin. The tin should be large enough to accommodate all the lemons in a single layer. Tuck the thyme under the lemons, then scatter over the sugar. Roast for 30 minutes.

Add the blueberries to the lemons along with 200 ml of the water. Roast for a further 25–30 minutes. The lemons should be slightly charred around the edges and the blueberries jammy. Set aside until cool to the touch. Press the roasted lemon flesh into the pan juices.

Scrape the fruit pulp into a sieve set over a large bowl. Press firmly to extract all the juices. Add the remaining 225 ml of water to the pulp and stir through. Strain once more, this time using a finer sieve or muslin cloth to clarify the liquid. Pour into sterilized bottles and seal.

Keep chilled until ready to use. Keeps well for up to 1 month, chilled.

TO RECONSTITUTE
60–80 ml lemonade cordial to 250 ml sparkling mineral water or soda water.

PLUM SHRUB WITH ROSEMARY & THYME

Shrubs are essentially vinegar-based syrups made by macerating fresh fruit, sugar and aromatics. Their concentrated flavour makes them ideal for cocktails and summer punch coolers. Raspberries, strawberries, blackberries and nectarines are lovely too.

MAKES 500 ML

- 400 g plums, washed and stoned
- 250 g granulated white sugar
- 2 sprigs of fresh rosemary
- 3 sprigs of fresh thyme
- 220 ml apple cider vinegar

Cut the plums into smallish pieces, 2–3 cm in size. Place in a non-reactive ceramic or glass bowl. Add the sugar, rosemary and thyme, then toss to coat the fruit. Cover the bowl with cling film and place in a cool corner of the kitchen for 24 hours.

Give the fruit a good mix. It should be syrupy and fragrant. Add the vinegar and stir through gently. Cover once more and set aside for another 24 hours.

On day three, transfer to the fridge and leave to macerate for 5–6 days.

Strain the syrup through a sieve, pressing lightly to extract the juices. To filter out the pulp, strain through a finer sieve or muslin cloth. Pour into a sterilized bottle and seal.

Chill in the fridge for 1 week before using to allow the flavours to develop.

Keeps well for up to 6 weeks, chilled.

TO RECONSTITUTE (TO TASTE)
Half fill a tumbler with ice. Add about 45 ml of the shrub and top up with sparkling mineral water, tonic water, soda or prosecco.

SHRUB COCKTAIL 1 part shrub, 1 part fresh juice, 2 parts spirits, top up with sparkling mineral water, tonic or prosecco.

SPEKBOOM GIN & TONIC

A perfect elixir on a hot summer's day, using local wonder-plant, Spekboom.

MAKES 1

60 ml gin
30 ml Spekboom Simple Syrup (page 266)
200 ml tonic water
lime slice, ice and a sprig of spekboom, to serve

Fill a highball glass with plenty of ice. Add the gin and spekboom syrup, and stir to combine.

Top up with the tonic water and 'lift' with a drink stirrer to retain as much of the fizz as possible.

Finish with lime slices and a botanical sprig.

KOMBUCHA PALOMA

Paloma, Spanish for 'dove', is a simple, straight-up tequila, lime and grapefruit-flavoured cocktail. Kombucha and prosecco add fresh complexity. And more bubbles. Cheerful and delicious.

SERVES 4–6

125 ml tequila
150 ml freshly squeezed ruby grapefruit juice, chilled
30 ml Rooibos & Honey Simple Syrup (page 266)
30 ml lime juice
500 ml rooibos kombucha, chilled
500 ml prosecco, chilled
thinly sliced ruby grapefruit and ice, to finish (optional)

In a large pitcher, combine the tequila, grapefruit juice, simple syrup and lime juice.

Add the kombucha and swirl gently. You want to retain the bubbles, if possible.

Pour into chilled glasses and top up with prosecco. Finish with thinly sliced ruby grapefruit and ice, if you like.

MANDARIN OLD FASHIONED

At first, robust and hard-hitting, settling to a lighter finish. The synergy between dark syrup and bourbon makes for a smooth, well-rounded mouthfeel. Fresh mandarin, although reformist, lends a mellow citrusy twist.

SERVES 1

5 ml Demerara Simple Syrup (page 266)
2 dashes Angostura bitters
30 ml freshly squeezed mandarin juice, strained
1 large ice cube
45 ml bourbon
mandarin peel

Add the Demerara Simple Syrup, bitters and mandarin juice to a tumbler, along with one large ice cube. Add the bourbon and stir until well chilled. Hold the mandarin peel over the cocktail and twist to express the oils, then place the peel over the rim of the glass and serve.

CARAMEL CREAM LIQUEUR

Smooth and rich, a sort of liquid velvet. The chocolate sauce recipe makes more than you'll need for one batch, although, if you're making it for end-of-year gifting, you may well use it up.

MAKES 900 ML

CHOCOLATE SAUCE
MAKES 300 ML

35 g cocoa powder
125 ml water
100 g granulated white sugar
1.25 ml Maldon sea salt flakes
5 ml vanilla extract
35 g dark chocolate (70%), roughly chopped
55 g milk chocolate (35%), roughly chopped
60 ml fresh cream

CARAMEL CREAM LIQUEUR
385 g Nestlé Caramel Treat
250 ml fresh cream
60 ml Chocolate Sauce
7.5 ml vanilla extract
5 ml espresso instant coffee powder combined with 10 ml warm water
300 ml whisky

START BY MAKING THE CHOCOLATE SAUCE. Place the cocoa and water in a saucepan and whisk to combine, breaking up any clumps. Add the sugar and salt. Bring slowly up to the boil. Simmer over a medium heat until the sugar is completely dissolved, and the sauce thickened, around 4 minutes.

Remove from the heat, then add the vanilla and both chopped chocolates. Whisk until melted, then add the cream and stir through. Pour into a sterilized bottle and set aside to cool.

FOR THE LIQUEUR, scrape the caramel into a blender. Add all the remaining ingredients and blend until smooth and creamy. Pour into a decanter and chill overnight.

Before serving, set on the counter to come to room temperature. Shake or stir the liqueur before pouring. Lovely neat or over crushed ice.

COOK'S NOTE: The chocolate sauce keeps well in the fridge for several weeks, ideal for impromptu sundaes.

SIMPLE SYRUPS

DEMRARA SIMPLE SYRUP

MAKES 150 ML

125 g dark demerara sugar
125 ml water

Place the sugar and water in a small saucepan. Bring slowly up to the boil. Simmer for 2–3 minutes until the sugar is completely dissolved. Set aside to cool. Pour into a sterilized bottle and seal. Keeps well for several months, chilled.

ROOIBOS & HONEY SIMPLE SYRUP

MAKES 160 ML

100 g light brown sugar
30 ml honey
125 ml freshly brewed rooibos tea

Place the sugar, honey and tea in a small saucepan. Bring slowly up to the boil. Simmer for 2–3 minutes until the sugar is completely dissolved. Set aside to cool. Pour into a sterilized bottle and seal. Keeps well for several months, chilled.

SPEKBOOM SYRUP

MAKES 160 ML

125 g white granulated sugar
250 ml water
spekboom stem, leaves plucked (125 ml yield)
1 lemon, skin-on, thinly sliced
30 ml lemon juice

Place the sugar, water, spekboom leaves, lemon slices and lemon juice in a small saucepan. Bring slowly up to the boil. Simmer for 10–12 minutes. Strain through a fine sieve and discard the solids. Set aside to cool. Pour into a sterilized bottle and seal. Keeps well for 3–4 weeks, chilled.

RUBY GRAPEFRUIT & BASIL SYRUP

Not quite a simple syrup, but spun with pink citrus juice and basil. If you're using it as a cordial, the ratio of syrup to water (sparkling or still) can vary between 1:3–1:4, depending on personal preference. The basil isn't loud, more an herbaceous flutter.

MAKES 400 ML

250 ml water
150 ml freshly squeezed ruby grapefruit juice
210 g granulated white sugar
20 g fresh basil leaves
zest of 1 lemon

Place all the ingredients in a small saucepan. Bring slowly up to the boil and simmer gently for 5 minutes. Set aside to infuse for around 30 minutes. Strain, then pour into a sterilized jar. Chill for up to a month.

GLOSSARY

Amasi – fermented milk, similar to plain yoghurt but slightly more tangy. Indigenous to South Africa and Lesotho.

Angostura bitters – an essential cocktail ingredient made from a blend of botanicals, herbs and spices. Technically an alcohol, although negligible when diluted.

Aquafaba – leftover liquid from tinned chickpeas.

Bucatini – similar to spaghetti, but thicker, with a signature hole running down the centre.

Burrata – soft cow's milk cheese with a mozzarella exterior and a fresh curd and cream centre.

Dolcelatte – made from cow's milk, milder in taste and sweeter than gorgonzola with a softer texture. Aged for 2–3 months.

Dukkah – Egyptian blend of nuts, seeds and spices. Often served with bread and olive oil, for dipping.

Edamame beans – whole, immature soya beans. High in protein. Popular in Asian cuisine.

Fattoush – a Middle Eastern salad, typically including lettuce, cucumber, radish, tomato, and crisp pita bread pieces.

Fior di latte – meaning 'flower of milk', indicating the best quality milk. A soft mozzarella made from cow's milk. Lighter flavour than buffalo mozzarella.

Gochujang – spicy paste used in Korean cooking, made from chillies, fermented soya beans, rice and salt.

Guajillo chilli – a mild Mexican chilli with a slightly sweet, bitter taste.

Harissa – Tunisian spice paste, popular in North African and Middle Eastern dishes.

Herbes de Provence – an aromatic combination of dried herbs typically used in Provençal dishes, with basil, thyme, rosemary, tarragon and lavender being key ingredients.

Kashmiri chilli powder – originating from Kashmir. Loved for its vibrant red colour and mild heat.

Kombucha – fermented drink made with tea, sugar, bacteria and yeast. Full of probiotics. Gut healthy.

Miso – fermented soya bean paste. Adds salty umami flavour to many Japanese dishes.

Nigella seeds – tiny black seeds with a subtle onion flavour.

Nutritional yeast – deactivated yeast, sold as a food product. Good source of vitamins, minerals and essential amino acids. Suitable cheese replacement in vegan cooking.

Pangrattato – oftentimes referred to as poor man's parmesan in Italian cuisine. Toasted breadcrumbs, flavoured with olive oil, salt and pepper. Much of the time herbs and garlic are added, too.

Panko breadcrumbs – Japanese breadcrumbs made from steamed crustless bread, which is flaked, then dried. Good for crunchy coatings.

Pecorino – hard Italian cheese made from sheep's milk. Similar to parmesan, but more tangy, sharp and salty with a granular texture.

Pomegranate syrup or molasses – made from pure pomegranate juice. Tart and sweet. Traditionally used in Middle Eastern cooking.

Prosecco vinegar – made from Italian prosecco with a pleasantly tart and fruity taste.

Rigatoni – short, wide pasta tubes, smooth on the inside and ridged on the outside.

Salamoia – a salted brine made with water, olive oil, salt and, sometimes, herbs. Poured over focaccia before baking.

Sichuan peppercorns – slight lemony taste, but no heat. Creates a tingling sensation. Commonly used in Asian cooking.

Sorghum – gluten-free ancient grain native to Africa.

Sumac – bright red, granular powder made from dried sumac berries. Tart and lemony. A staple of Middle Eastern and Mediterranean cuisine.

Tamarind – widely used in Indian and Thai cooking. Very tart with a citrusy flavour and deep molasses-like colour.

Tangzhong – a cooked roux made with water and flour. Used in breadmaking to yield a soft-textured bread. Also promotes an extended shelf life.

Tipo 00 – finest grade of milled flour in Italy, also known as Italian Double Zero. The gold standard for pizza and pasta dough.

Za'atar – Middle Eastern spice blend made with dried thyme, oregano, sumac and toasted sesame seeds.

CONVERSION CHARTS

MILLILITRES	CUPS
60 ml	¼ cup
80 ml	⅓ cup
125 ml	½ cup
160 ml	⅔ cup
180 ml	¾ cup
250 ml	1 cup
500 ml	2 cups
750 ml	3 cups
1 litre	4 cups

MEASURING SPOONS

1.25 ml	¼ teaspoon
2.5 ml	½ teaspoon
3.75 ml	¾ teaspoon
5 ml	1 teaspoon
10 ml	2 teaspoons
15 ml	1 tablespoon

OVEN TEMPERATURES

Celsius	Fahrenheit
110°C	225°F
120°C	250°F
140°C	275°F
150°C	300°F
160°C	325°F
180°C	350°F
190°C	375°F
200°C	400°F
220°C	425°F
230°C	450°F

FREQUENTLY USED INGREDIENT CONVERSIONS

150 g cake wheat flour	250 ml
150 g bran-rich self-raising flour	250 ml
150 g white bread flour	250 ml
100 g rye flour	250 ml
130 g wholegrain spelt flour	250 ml
120 g almond flour	250 ml
220 g granulated white sugar	250 ml
220 g castor sugar	250 ml
160 g icing sugar	250 ml
125 g butter – ½ cup plus	15 ml
50 g parmesan, grated	125 ml
60 g cheddar cheese, grated	125 ml
140 g whole rolled oats	250 ml
120 g porridge oats	250 ml
100 g desiccated coconut	250 ml
200 g uncooked rice	250 ml
200 g bulgur wheat	250 ml
180 g uncooked quinoa	250 ml
100 g fresh breadcrumbs	250 ml
150 g almonds	250 ml
120 g walnuts	250 ml
75 g sunflower seeds	125 ml
80 g pumpkin seeds	125 ml
60 g sesame seeds	125 ml
75 g raisins/sultanas	125 ml

REPLACEMENT VALUES

1 egg white	replace with 30 ml aquafaba (chickpea liquid) for a vegan alternative
1 whole egg	replace with 15 ml flaxseed meal combined with 45 ml cold water

FLOUR FIXES

self-raising flour	substitute with 150 g cake wheat flour plus 5 ml baking powder
bran-rich self-raising flour	substitute with 150 g self-raising flour plus 15 g digestive bran

INGREDIENT EQUIVALENTS

PRODUCE

aubergine	eggplant, brinjal
baby marrow	courgette, zucchini
chickpeas	garbanzo beans
coriander	cilantro
pumpkin seeds	pepitas
rocket	arugula
spring onion	scallion
sweet red pepper	capsicum

BAKING INGREDIENTS

cake wheat flour	all-purpose cake flour
cornflour	cornstarch, maizena
farina tipo 00	Italian double zero flour
icing sugar	confectioner's sugar, powdered sugar

INDEX

ACKNOWLEDGEMENTS

Firstly, to you the reader, the home cook, supporter of good food and print. If it weren't for you, books such as this one would not be possible. And what a shame that would be. For me, cookbooks are a wonderland of places I long to visit and the food I dream of eating.

To Darren, my constant, thank you for choosing to walk the road less travelled with me. You've taught me to be tenacious and brave. How lucky I am. When you proposed and I said no, thank you for not leaving. And when I said I couldn't imagine spending the next 50 years with you, still you waited. Now, I think 50 years may not be enough.

Kyles and Bree, thank you for the magic you bring to my life. The hysterical laughter and weeping, each in equal measure, the dishwashing, ingredient shops, furniture moving and lifters of back-breaking marble slabs. It seems the apple may just have fallen closer to the tree than you'd like. I love you to the moon and back. When I visit your homes one day, I hope there'll be cake. And Skylar, no box mixes please.

Annalize, your commitment to detail and patience is a gift! You are a true talent. Thank you for whipping my mishaps into shape.

To Bev, my publisher. From our very first online conversation, I knew you'd get things done. You're on your game, undeterred by the challenges and obstacles that come with publishing cookbooks. Thank you for your constant support and making the process infinitely easier.

Thank you to my editor, Linda, for creating order and a sensible flow throughout. With an eye for detail and masterful command of language, it's been so comforting having you in my corner.

To Helen, my designer. I don't know quite how to thank you. Your patience and skill at arrangement, placing and crafting solutions is nothing short of genius. You're one of a kind.

To Aimee, for mapping the way forward, from start to finish. Managing the micro and macro aspects of production is no easy feat! Thank you for taking the reins and being an expert juggler.

Published in 2024 by Penguin Books,
an imprint of Penguin Random House
South Africa (Pty) Ltd
Company Reg. No. 1953/000441/07
The Estuaries, 4 Oxbow Crescent,
Century Avenue, Century City, 7441
PO Box 1144, Cape Town, 8000, South Africa

Reprinted in 2024

www.penguinrandomhouse.co.za

ISBN 978-1-48590-162-4

PUBLISHER: Beverley Dodd
MANAGING EDITOR: Aimee Sinclair
EDITOR: Linda de Villiers
DESIGNER: Helen Henn
PROOFREADER: Anita van Zyl
PHOTOGRAPHY: Dianne Bibby
FOOD PREPARATION: Dianne Bibby
PROP AND FOOD STYLING: Dianne Bibby
AUTHOR IMAGE: Annalize Nel

Reproduction: Studio Repro

Printed and bound in China by Golden Prosperity Printing and Packaging (Heyuan) Co., Ltd